Saving Face in China

Saving Face in China

A First-Hand Guide For Any Traveller To China

Anne-Laure Monfret

Copyright © 2011 by Anne-Laure Monfret.

Photograph by Julian Okwu

Illustrated by Mélanie Abellan

Library of Congress Control Number:		2011904529
ISBN:	Hardcover	978-1-4568-9064-3
	Softcover	978-1-4568-9063-6
	Ebook	978-1-4568-9065-0

This book was printed in the United States of America.

To order additional copies of this book, contact:
Xlibris Corporation
1-888-795-4274
www.Xlibris.com
Orders@Xlibris.com
96492

Contents

For anyone wishing to travel, do business, or take up residence in China, this book provides an indispensable tool for understanding the "Chinese" way of thinking. For everyone else, the book offers an insightful and entertaining window into one of the world's most frequently misunderstood cultures.

—Ellen Orr, American resident in China for 15 years, former manager of an investment banking joint venture.

Through many anecdotes and experiences of both Chinese and Western people, Anne-Laure Monfret shows how an understanding of the culture, customs and practices of China is valuable in preventing loss of face and achieving "win-win" situations. Carefully researched, this book gives an insight into the importance of face in China, an understanding of which is necessary in dealings with Chinese citizens. It is useful for all Western people who want to do business in China.

—Andrew Ritchie, General Manager of Total Petrochemicals in Great Britain/Sales manager in China from 1997 to 2005 (spent 16 years in Asia).

Any Westerner arriving in China for the first time will experience their fair share of surprises and misunderstandings. Although we all know that every effort must be made to avoid causing face-loss to the Chinese, few know much how to handle it. Calling on genuine personal accounts, anecdotes and experiences which she has gathered together and analysed over several years, Anne-Laure Monfret gives us the keys to understanding the sometimes enigmatic and often surprising attitudes and reactions of the Chinese. This book is an invaluable tool for understanding the Chinese mind-set and an essential travelling companion for those seeking to conquer the Chinese market as well as those interested in exploring the subtleties of a culture which sometimes seems a world away from their own.

—Pierre Shan, managing director of Onduline China and Franco-Chinese mediator/speaker for the French Chamber of Commerce and Industry in China.

Introduction

A person needs a face like a tree needs bark.
Chinese proverb

Why write a book about the notion of face in China?

Most foreigners who live in China or are about to be sent there have already heard about the Chinese notion of face. With more and more businesses expanding to China and new partnerships being formed between Chinese companies and their international counterparts, learning how to deal with Chinese has become paramount. Open any book on China and the concept of face will come up somewhere.

"This is undoubtedly the most curious aspect of Chinese psychology; It is abstract, intangible and the most subtle of models which govern Chinese inter-social relations," writes Lin Yutang, the prominent Chinese author of "My country and my people."

"Face, or *mianzi*, is arguably one of the three key motivators that govern behavior in the PRC these days, the others being money and power. But the three are related," writes Scott D. Seligman in "Chinese Business Etiquette."

Although most foreigners have heard of this notion, only few can define precisely what it is:

"Like everyone I keep hearing about face and especially the expression "losing face," says a Westerner, "but if you ask me what face actually means in China, I honestly couldn't tell you!"

A Canadian consultant of Chinese descent who advises foreign companies on how to do business in China makes the following observation:

"The degree of misapprehension that exists over the notion of face is striking. I've often asked foreign managers: 'What does the Chinese notion of face mean to you?' and I've received all kinds of answers. For instance, I was once told: 'In China, you have to demonstrate to your business partner that he is more important than you to give him face.' These short-cut interpretations are the cause of many misunderstandings between foreign business people and Chinese entrepreneurs."

Face is constantly being referred to in China and paradoxically many foreigners that live or work in China still find it hard to understand the implications that face evokes. That is what lead me to write this book.

Although the notion of face is often badly interpreted, it doesn't necessarily means that it is some sort of mysterious and incomprehensible phenomenon of Chinese culture which can only be grasped by the Chinese themselves.

The Scottish vice-chairman of an international group has his own, rather humorous view on this:

"When the Chinese tell me that as a foreigner I can't understand the notion of face, I usually reply: 'You know saving face is important to us, too. When I play golf with a potential business partner in Scotland I have to let him win to save him from losing face.' How much you actually believe it, is not the issue. The point is that the notion of face does not only exist in China."

This book helps to demystify the concept of face while highlighting its importance in everyday life in China.

What does "face" represent in China?

In Europe or the United States of America the expression "losing face" means losing prestige by tolerating an attack on one's honor, dignity and reputation. This notion, or phrase, was in fact borrowed from the Chinese and only became part of the English language in the late 19th century. At that point it had already existed in China for several centuries and had established itself in many different shapes and forms. The notion of prestige for example, has only existed in China since the Tang dynasty (7th-10th century AD), while others had been around for much longer (like the notion of politeness). It should therefore hardly come as a surprise that our perception of "losing face" varies considerably from the perception of the Chinese.

The Chinese say "he lost face" like we might say "he got upset" or "it really hurt his ego." This is at least how many Westerners tend to view the concept of face.

❖ More than just pride

Although there is some truth in that, face cannot be reduced to pride alone. Moreover, Chinese people—when questioned about face—mention many other aspects before ever even touching upon this aspect of personal slight.

Here some of their examples:

- "If somebody refuses to drink with you, you lose face; if an acquaintance sees you in the streets and does not greet you, that means you do not have face; if your decision is questioned in front of others, what a loss of face; if your child is not amongst the top ten students of his class, you lose face; if you are poor, you do not have a face. All problems in China are related to face."

- "The notion of face is in our blood. It comes from our education, it is in our tradition, our culture, our mentality."

- "Having face is to be recognized by others through your social status, your appearance and your material possessions. They are all signs that show you succeeded in your life, personally or through others (your children, your parents, your country). Losing your face is when you lose all that."

❖ A social notion

Face goes beyond the individual notion. It is also and above all a social notion. In fact, face is inseparable from position and social image. If you cause somebody to lose face you do not only hurt him personally or in his pride, but you also risk that he loses his standing in the eyes of others. And this is where a loss of face becomes very serious, especially considering that in Chinese society both social status and public image are extremely important (conversely, social failure is a great shame).

The Chinese word for face is *mianzi* (面 子) or *lian* (脸) which literally means "visage." "Once a Chinese loses face, the others will completely ignore him, to them he becomes faceless, he becomes a stranger," says a Chinese. "To lose face is like ceasing to exist in the eyes of others and in society."

❖ A question of relationships

Face is also a question of relationships, an aspect that is of utmost importance in China. The Chinese spend a lot of time looking after their relationships. As a result, saving the face of others is just as important to the Chinese as saving their own. This is particularly true in negotiations, when you must always make sure no one loses face if you want to get to an agreement.

Face is a form of mutual respect, diplomacy, politeness and a way of living, which above all aims at maintaining good relationships. Not giving face to somebody is considered ill-mannered and disrespectful. Imagine a Chinese talking about his last trip to France over dinner to try and make conversation with the French sitting next him. He makes a mistake about where a certain city is situated. The French man cannot help but correct him: "No, no, you got that wrong. This city is in the north of France, not in the south." So what would the man have done wrong?

- he would have made his Chinese neighbor lose face in front of everybody;

- he would have ruined the relationship the Chinese had tried to kindle.

And all that just to make a point that was not really worth the effort. The Chinese only tried to give himself face (by showing that he had travelled abroad) and to find common interests to establish a relationship. It was a question of face and relationship, not a geography lesson!

Relationships are a top priority in China and those who do not understand this are bound to fail. A German explains:

> "What really counts in Germany is the technical quality of products and services. We don't need to yell *gan bei* (drinking toast) or sing our hearts out at karaoke night to sell our products. *'Arbeit ist Arbeit; Schnaps ist Schnaps!'* In other words 'there's a time for work and a time to drink and have fun.'
>
> In my country I can do excellent business with someone I don't particularly get on with. Above all I judge the quality of the service and the product. It is pretty obvious that in China relationships are much more important than know-how or results.
>
> A fantastic product and quality service is always appreciated but to the Chinese this doesn't count as much as a good relationship.
>
> In China you have to go to the restaurant and yell *gan bei* all night, it's all part of the job. The magic word there is relationship."

What are the goals of this guide?

❖ Learn from other people's experiences

In China, I conducted a hundred interviews with both Chinese and foreigners including French, American, British, Italian, German and Spanish nationals, and asked them about their personal intercultural experiences.

In one of the interviews I conducted over a casual dinner a foreigner told me:

> "It feels good to be able to share our experiences and to discover that others have been confronted with the same issues and difficulties.

Suddenly you feel less alone and cannot stop laughing about the things that happened to you over the years."

Along the same lines, a British man who had just set up his own company in China confided to me:

"There is always a degree of malicious joy when you realize that others have made the same mistakes. I love China, but there are days when I feel like throwing the towel because everybody and everything gets on my nerves. A book on the mistakes and *faux-pas* made by others would have cheered me up big time."

This book is not just a "do or don't" guide neither a scientific paper on the concept of face. It is full of personal stories and cultural blunders committed both by people who are new to China and those who are long-standing foreign residents. This will allow you to reflect upon the experience of others, to learn from it and, last but not least, to have a good read.

❖ Help you to work out what is going on around you

Not everything can be explained by the concept of face, but understanding how it works can prevent many misunderstandings.

"Once you have understood what face means to a Chinese, you'll suddenly understand so much more about the way the Chinese think. If you haven't assimilated this notion of face, then it is difficult to get the rest," says a French woman whom it took several years to even get to grips with the modus operandi of her Chinese husband.

Understanding the concept of face enables us to get an insight into a big part of Chinese culture, as the two are closely linked. Face can help us understand certain behavioral patterns, certain reactions and typical situations in business or private life which had previously seemed absurd.

However, it is important to steer clear of stereotypes. Even if it seems like it at first sight, it is wrong to assume that all Chinese behave the same way. A Chinese manager in his 50s who lived through the Great Cultural Revolution will behave differently from somebody in his 20s who speaks fluent English, just got out of university and only knows times of economic boom and prosperity. Similarly, the reaction of Mr Li, who was born and raised in Beijing and whose life and values are based on Confucius, is likely to be the complete opposite of Mr Wang, a Shanghai businessman who is very open to the outside world and for whom financial interests are likely to be more important than the questions of face.

❖ **Introduce to you the most important aspects of etiquette and code of conduct in China**

In China, etiquette is inseparable from the notion of face. Even though it is not necessary for foreigners to follow the etiquette and rules of behavior as strictly as the locals, the Chinese are very appreciative of foreigners who understand and respect some of them. To know the basics will help you to cultivate positive relationships with the Chinese and give them face.

Ultimately face is a vital part of everyday life in China and most of the issues between foreigners and Chinese can be eliminated by understanding the concept and paying it the outmost attention. To help you in your communication with the Chinese is the main purpose of this book.

Introduction: Brainteaser—Test your knowledge

Check the right answers

1. **Face is:**

   a. a phenomenon strictly reserved for the Chinese.
   b. universal.
   c. only an invention of the Chinese to make foreigners feel insecure.

   Answer: b. universal. The concept of face is neither strictly reserved for the Chinese nor exclusive to any other Asian country. In fact nobody, whether Chinese or European or American, likes losing face. Any foreigner, just like any Chinese, dislikes being questioned or yelled at in public. We all try to protect our dignity and fear being embarrassed in front of others.

   However, even though the notion of face is universal, it still has a special place in Chinese society and culture. As John L. Chan, author of "China Streetsmart" put it: "Face is not so different in kind, but certainly in degree."

2. **Face can be compared to:**

   a. a mask.
   b. a shopwindow.
   c. a mirror.

   Answer: All three. All three words are based on the Chinese word *mian* 面 (face).
   A mask is *mianju* 面 具, such as the mask from the opera in Beijing, i.e. the social mask we wear when facing others.

   Mian is also used for the front of a store (*dianmian* 店 面), or the facade of a building (*zhengmian* 正 面). In a way, face is like a facade we keep up in order to hide what is inside. It is a way of dressing up reality to protect our reputation.

   In addition to that, *mian* means mirror (*mian jingzi* 面 镜 子). It reflects the fact that the Chinese define their own value according to what others see in them. Face is our image reflected, thus mirrored by society. The Chinese live through the perceptions of others. As a result they worry a lot about what others think: *"Bie ren zenme shuo?"* (What might other people say?) or *"Bie ren zenme xiang?"* (What will other people think?).

3. Can face be compared to honor?

    a. Yes.
    b. No.

Answer: Yes and no. Face is somewhat related to honor but should not be confused with questions of honor prevalent in Europe or the United States (and even less so with the Japanese tradition of *hara-kiri*). I posed this question to a Chinese director, a former student of Political Science in France:

Q: Can face be compared to honor?

A: I don't think so. It is certainly different from the way honor is understood in Western countries. Abandoning the battlefield when you are out-numbered or out-gunned, for example, is not considered a loss of face in China.

Q: A Japanese woman told me that during World War II Japanese mothers would encourage their sons to join the war to give the family face. Not that they wanted them to die, but being unwilling to die for your country caused the family to lose face. Are there similar notions in China?

A: Actually, I don't think so. We have some national heroes but they are few. Take Lei Feng for instance, a foot soldier who loyally served his people and who is often featured in Chinese propaganda. His example is prominent but still conflicts with Chinese culture and the mentality of most Chinese.

"My Country and My People" written by Lin Yutang in the 1930s, picks up on this notion: "The "yellow peril" may arrive from Japan, but it will certainly not come from China. Our deepest instinct is to die for our family, not for our country. There is not a single man amongst us who would be willing to sacrifice his life to save the world."

4. **In which of the following situations do you risk causing a Chinese to lose face?**

    a. Categorically refusing to take face seriously whenever you deal with the Chinese.
    b. Commiting an action that question the authority of a superior.
    c. Criticizing somebody in public.
    d. Mentioning over and over again that somebody made a mistake.
    e. Refusing to drink and toast during a business dinner.
    f. Offering a fake Rolex worth 60 RMB (6 euros/ 10 USD) to your client.
    g. Using irony.
    h. Looking down on somebody.

Answer: All of the above. These situations correspond with the **eight most common mistakes** foreigners make, all of which are described in detail in this book.

I did not choose the number **8** arbitrarily; in fact, in China, **8** is a lucky number. In Mandarin "eight" is *ba*, but in Cantonese it is pronounced like *fa*, which means "to make a fortune."

People would do anything to have parking spaces or apartment numbers containing the number **8**. Mobile phone numbers containing lots of **8**s are more expensive than regular numbers. The phone number **8 888 88 88** was sold for more than two million Yuan (about 200,000 euros/ 300,000 USD) in a public bid. The buyer, Sichuan Airlines, is highly satisfied with its purchase and their customers now enjoy calling them even more. It is not a coincidence that the famous Jin Mao tower in Shanghai has **88** floors. Also, it was not surprising that the opening ceremony of the Olympic Games in Beijing took place on **August 8, 2008** and started at **08:08:08 pm**.

So how could I have chosen another number for this book?

Chapter 1

Take face seriously

A single word can wreck a deal.
Chinese proverb

Some foreigners simply pay no attention to face and most underestimate its power. Either they are convinced that face is some sort of urban myth or they acknowledge its existence but expect the Chinese to adapt to the foreign culture.

This kind of attitude can be risky and in some cases also very costly.

A French woman remembers a disastrous experience which involved a fellow colleague who had just arrived in China:

"We spent years trying to build a working partnership with several Chinese institutions. In China, everything is founded on a system of relationships and the cultivation of trust. Even such bureaucratic things as requests for legal permits and authorizations largely depend on this. A Chinese colleague supported us the entire time and used her close contacts with senior figures in the industry to help us out.

Then our new colleague arrived from France. Being fresh on the scene she decided to bypass this key player. The new colleague considered this person to be of little value to us and our enterprise. She made our Chinese colleague lose face. And even though the

Chinese colleague kept her feelings under wraps it was clear to all of us that she was going to undo everything behind our backs in order to clear her name.

One little misstep by my impatient French colleague had destroyed 15 years worth of ground work and cost us a promising business relationship."

Confucius was right when he said:

"A trifling impatience will confound a great project!"

The concept of efficiency

Chinese and Westerners do not share the same concept of efficiency.

In our hemisphere efficiency is based on an action that is expected to produce a direct result. Efficiency gains need to have immediate impact and change the course of current events.

In China, efficiency is based on the belief that it is indirect effects which are most powerful. Efficiency gains take place over time and are expected to blend into the course of events.

Example: Imagine a company that has a serious problem to resolve and the only person capable of providing this solution is Mr. Shan.

- Scenario 1: Mr. Pang invites Mr. Shan for the weekend but waits until the end of his stay to raise the subject. He praises Mr. Shan's expertise and assures him of his unshakeable belief in his skills. So Mr. Pang takes time to develop a good strategy and focuses on how to solve the problem on the long run.
- Scenario 2: Mr. Taylor organizes an urgent meeting. He brings up the problem immediately and urges Mr. Shan to come up with a solution as soon as possible. Mr. Tayor expects the paper to be on his desk the following week and instructs Mr. Shan to implement the changes promptly after the proposal has been accepted.

The question is not so much who has been the most efficient—since that will depend on the situation—but appreciating that there is more than one way of being efficient.

Causing somebody to lose face is risky

❖ The more important the person, the greater the risk you take

Say you cause an employee to lose face, but believe he can be easily replaced anyway. Or you cause your housekeeper to lose face, but were planning to fire her anyway. Or you cause a street vendor to lose face, but know you will never see him again. None of this is particularly nice, but at least there will not be any major consequences. However, if you cause certain key figures in your Chinese environment to lose face, you or your business could be exposed to serious risk.

- if you cause an important employee you just trained for six painful months to lose face, you can be sure to be training his or her replacement for the six months to come.
- causing your best salesman to lose face can impact your company performance either by sudden and seemingly inexplicable drops in sales or because he walks straight out on you.
- causing a landlord who rents you a furnished house to lose face means you risk finding your home emptied of its contents when you get home from work (this actually occurred!).
- if you cause an important government official to lose face then you may end up having to close your business (provided you have had the chance to open it in the first place).

A Chinese businessman tells how a major US company lost 10 million dollars:

"During talks with the Chinese authorities for an investment, a US firm demanded that its name be shown on the building. The authorities refused. They allowed the company to display its name inside the offices but they did not want it going up on the building itself. The Americans kept arguing. They failed to realize that trying to convince a Chinese official to take back his decision was tantamount to causing him a loss of face. He had said 'no' and challenging his decision was like questioning his credibility.

For the Chinese administration, face counts more than anything money can buy. The Americans eventually retreated when they realized that they were getting themselves into serious trouble. But it was already too late and in the end the American company lost the entire contract."

Weigh up what is at stake before you act or say something that could cause a Chinese to lose face.

❖ **Never discount people who appear "insignificant"**

You never really know from the get-go who is a key player and who only a "small fish."

"I'm sure my boss will never forget one of his first negotiations in China," says a Chinese employee who worked for a foreign company. "A woman who'd just served the tea asked him during the meeting if everything was okay or whether he needed anything. He didn't pay much attention to her. Then it turned out that she was in fact the company director, the key decision-maker. My boss didn't have a clue."

This is a major lesson when dealing with the Chinese: never judge a book by its cover.

Marie Chantal Piques, author of "The Mirrors of Negotiations in China," recounts the story of a French managing director who only came up with a disdainful, "Oh, right . . ." when the Chinese director introduced him to the humble workshop manager. Little did he know that she was the director's wife, a very important figure in any Chinese family business.

Before causing somebody to lose face, make sure you know who you are dealing with.

Spilt water is hard to retrieve

In European culture embarrassing moments are laughed about and soon forgotten. A loss of face in Great Britain or France is easily restored. The same goes for the United States. In China, on the other hand, it is all very different.

❖ Difficult to repair

An American who worked both in the United States and in Poland compares China with both countries:

"In the States, it's perfectly ok for someone to say 'I think that's a bad idea!' right in the middle of a meeting. It's being discussed and taken into the consideration. And if it turns out that he was wrong, the same guy will easily back down by saying: 'Ok, ok, I got that wrong.' It isn't a problem because five minutes later everybody has forgotten already about it.

In Poland, it is less common to take somebody on in a meeting but I've seen it happening. You can always apologize afterwards in a one-to-one meeting. It's between you and the other person and resolved in what is perceived as a grown up conversation.

However, making this kind of a comment in a meeting in China is unthinkable. If you ever go down that road you'll struggle to repair the damage. By causing a Chinese to lose face you not only have to repair the relationship between the two of you, but also between him and the others (since they will look at him in a different way now that he's lost face), and between you and the others (who will have found your public criticizm very disrespectful)."

In American and European culture you always get a chance to take back what you said, but the Chinese do not have the luxury of this exit strategy. In China everything is much more complicated.

In Western countries for example, you can have a massive row with someone and then end up going for a beer or coffee afterwards. This, again, would be unthinkable in China.

As one Chinese recalls:

"I once saw two French colleagues have a fierce argument in the office corridor. One started criticizing the other's work shouting it from the top of his lungs. Everyone could hear what he was saying.

What amazed me was to see the two of them shortly afterwards sitting at a table eating with other colleagues and chatting away as if nothing had happened. If I had been publicly criticized that way I would have come up with a pretext to go have lunch somewhere else."

You may have long forgotten about the loss of face you caused, but your Chinese counterpart will still feel crushed.

❖ **Doing nothing about it**

Imagine you have just caused a Chinese to lose face. It is almost guaranteed that this was not the first time and that it will not be your last. So surely you must be wondering what you can do to help him or her to "regain" face? It may seem disappointing, but the truth is that there is not much you can do, really. In fact, an attempt to do so could backfire badly.

Desperately trying to save the situation is like digging yourself an even deeper hole.

"The best thing you can do is to never talk about it again. He lost face once; talking about it means he will lose face a second time," explains a European entrepreneur who worked in China for 20 years.

"You want to make up for it? You should have thought of that before you brought him into this mess. The Chinese know perfectly well that the situation is almost impossible to reverse which is why they pay so much attention to face in the first place. You can always try to apologize but in reality it would be like adding salt to the wound," adds a French executive.

However, according to this European human resources director, there is one feasible approach:

"I once caused a Chinese manager to lose face in a meeting. He held it against me for a long time. He is a very capable manager whom I respect, and to restore his face I felt I had to go to great lengths to make up for what I had done. So I took any chance I got to praise him and demonstrate in front of others that I thought that he was a competent and highly respectable decision-maker. This helped him win back some face."

Seek out opportunities to give your Chinese partner the chance to regain some face.

❖ Restoring the balance publicly

In the event of a major *faux-pas* or if you decide the circumstances are particularly serious, a public apology can be a means to saving the situation. At the same time you need to be sure about how to present your apology, otherwise it will be worthless.

The Chinese director of an industrial plant explains:

"I'm willing to put up with the fact that someone has caused me to lose face. But for the balance to be restored he must bend over backwards or accept a gesture which causes him to lose face in return, for instance presenting his sincere apologies. This must always be done in a very formal manner and in front of those who witnessed my initial loss of face."

Although this may seem somewhat humiliating (and it truly is, or else it would have no value to your Chinese partner), it is just one more part of the "face game."

A Chinese general manager gives a concrete example:

"Not long ago, my driver took the company car for personal use, which is strictly prohibited. By failing to comply with the corporate rules which I had established, he brought my credibility into question (and that of the company which I represent). My Chinese assistants suggested that I ask him to present a written apology to the company which he would then read out publicly in a meeting. This is standard practice in China. In other words, he had to agree to lose some face to restore my credibility."

Although this is a possibility, it is far from being a guarantee for success. A French boss remembers:

"I was once involved in a situation where we showed a pretty blatant lack of tact.

I was accompanying representatives of a major French company on a business trip to a Chinese province. They had come to check whether the business environment was compatible with their projects. All kinds of dignitaries had been lined up to meet us: local authorities, port customs, a quality office, delegations, etc. It had been decided that everyone would dine together as is the custom in China. We had barely arrived when we told them we would have to leave at 4 pm, using the feeble pretext that the company manager was suffering from a stomach ache.

Naturally, I apologized to everybody there and even sent them a letter, but they never replied. The damage had been done and there was nothing that I could have done to regain their trust.

This made me realize that I would have zero credibility in this province for the rest of my life. There is no way I could ever turn up there again."

Would the Chinese have replied to his letter had he found the right words?

An incident involving the United States and China demonstrates the importance of choosing the right words when presenting apologies to the Chinese:

On 1st April 2001 a US spy plane was forced to land on the Chinese island of Hainan following a collision with a Chinese fighter plane. The Chinese took the 24 crew members into custody and kept the spy plane.

The Chinese authorities then demanded a formal apology from the United States. The American President at the time, Georges W. Bush, sent a letter expressing his "regrets" (*yihan*) to the wife of the pilot who had died in the accident. Colin Powell, then Secretary of State, said he was "sorry" (*baoqian* in Chinese). While both statements seemed sincere and appropriate to Americans, China's President Jiang Zemin repeated his request for an apology saying that mere "regrets" were "unacceptable."

Regrets or *yihan* in Chinese are perceived as a lot less meaningful than the kind of apology expected and demanded by Beijing. The word *yihan* is used when something happens which is not your fault. *Baoqian* means you are generally sorry, for instance if you arrive late to a meeting. Whereas *daoqian* means you are apologizing for having done something wrong. It is understood as the acceptance of responsibility for what happened.

    The incident on the island of Hainan could have had serious consequences had Washington not replaced "we are sorry" with "we are *really* sorry" which seemed to mollify Beijing in the absence of the more substantial *daoqian*.

    After eleven days of tensions between the United States and China the diplomatic crisis was peacefully resolved.

If you apologize to somebody, apologize properly.

Do not pretend to be more Chinese than the Chinese

Even though it is risky not to take face seriously, it is also important not to go to the other extreme. Attributing too much importance to the concept of face can have equal drawbacks.

❖ You are not Chinese

By tirelessly trying to save everybody's face, many foreigners end up losing their patience, which ironically often results in a loss of face for those around them.

To avoid falling for this, a European woman who worked in China for seven years came up with his own safety valve:

"I pay careful attention to face at work, especially when there's a lot at stake. However, I tend to pay less attention in day-to-day encounters in shops or on the streets. You can't always keep a lid on your emotions. You need to let off steam every now and then otherwise you are bound to go mad."

Even Chinese acknowledge this point:

"Far too many Chinese think about face from morning to night without giving it a break. They get so worked up about face that they go to bed at night completely exhausted," says a Chinese taxi driver.

If saving face is exhausting to the Chinese, it is even more tiring for foreigners. Trying to follow the rules every day is like walking on eggshells. The solution here is simple but powerful: do not try to act like a Chinese and avoid playing a role that is not in line with your personality.

An American woman recounts her initial strategy:

"When I first arrived in China, I was really direct, probably too direct for the Chinese. When I had something on my mind I just went ahead and said it without thinking of the problems I might cause my employees or whether or not I was causing them to lose face.

I soon realized that this management style was not working well, so I did a complete u-turn. I totally changed my strategy and began to pay close attention to face. I was excessively polite and took care not to upset the Chinese who worked for me. Sadly this didn't get me anywhere either. I didn't manage to improve my relationship to the employees this way and on top of that I felt uncomfortable and unhappy.

In the end I decided to remain true to myself and stick to my trademark style. These days I am still very direct but I have fine-tuned it to make it a little bit more in line with the Chinese culture."

Keep an eye on face but be yourself, too.

❖ **You have your dignity and authority to defend**

Being overly cautious about face can be as damaging as ignoring it.

This Chinese businesswoman shares her thoughts about foreigners who take it too far:

> "Before they arrive here, some foreigners attend courses where they learn how to pay careful attention to the concept of face. But for some of them, it turns into an obsession.
>
> For instance, I remember working on a project which was in danger of falling behind schedule. The Chinese technicians kept doing it their way though, totally ignoring the advice of the foreign technicians.
>
> Determined not to come across as trying to impose their opinion on the Chinese, the foreign technicians told them: 'Our consultants have made a couple of suggestions on how to improve the process even further, but obviously it is up to you whether or not you decide to take their advice.' Needless to say, that the Chinese took them up on their invitation and carried on as before.
>
> So while it is important to pay attention to face and to address your Chinese partners in a polite way, it is also important to do this on the basis of the precise objectives you intend to achieve. Be polite, but also be firm and clear about what you want."

Mind you, the Chinese do not always follow their own rules and have been known to sometimes take even less care than foreigners. A Frenchman, who will probably never forget how a Chinese person caused him to lose face on his first days in China, recalls the following incident:

> "Before I left France, I was strongly advised to pay careful attention to face when dealing with the Chinese.

Mr. Wang was an exclusive agent for a French company, which, in fact, had appointed me to replace him. They were demoting him to a lower position, so you can imagine that Mr. Wang was not too pleased about my arrival. To him I was basically the enemy who had to be eliminated by all means and he did not hold back to underming my credibility whenever he got the chance. It was obvious to me that he was trying to win back his position but he also aimed at deliberately causing me to lose face in order to regain his own in the eyes of the others.

He would criticize my work in meetings and accuse me of being the source of every problem that crossed our way. He even sent a nasty letter about me to our senior management. He started investigating my private life and that of my Chinese girlfriend (the fact that we were not married was viewed with suspicion).

I have worked in other countries in Asia, in the United States and some Arab countries, but I've never come across such fierce determination to cause someone else to lose face.

Normally, in China, you don't criticize someone else in public. You don't bypass anybody. You do all you can to avoid conflict. In short, you do everything to prevent someone else from losing face, but in my case the opposite was true.

I just kept my mouth shut to make sure things wouldn't get even worse. Had I followed my instincts straight away I would have taken fewer precautions and not wasted so much time and energy on trying to save his face. When I realized that my silence only edged him on even further I had enough and joined his little game: I called him up and threatened him not to take it any further. This actually worked and he stopped giving me a hard time. In the end, I informed our senior management about everything, and looking at the evidence they were soon on my side. My predecessor lost his job then and there.

The lesson I learned from this is that yes, you should adapt to the country's culture and yes, you should pay attention to face. That does not, however, mean that you should let people walk all over you."

Although this case seems rather extreme, it is by no means an isolated incident. Many foreigners find it very difficult to protect themselves in these types of situations when they are fully aware that they will cause their Chinese counterparts to lose face. However, it is important to understand that trying to pay careful attention to face does not mean that you cannot display your authority. And it sure does not mean that others are allowed to treat you with disrespect. You also have a face, so do not hesitate to defend it.

> *If a Chinese takes it too far, do not worry about protecting his face.*

❖ **You have economic imperatives**

An American sales director who worked for a Chinese joint venture for a number of years says:

"It often seems that in China, saving people's face is more important than achieving economic efficiency.

One day a member of my sales team came to see me because a client had asked for a special clause to be added to his contract. I told him to get someone in the legal department to have a look at it.

'What do you want me to do?' he asked, confused.

Since I have made the experience that many of the communication problems are due to language, I repeated the instruction, speaking very slowly: 'Go call the legal assistant and ask her if this clause is legal.' This truly seemed to be beyond his comprehension. So I asked: 'What on earth were you planning to do?'

He said, 'I thought you were going to ask the director of the legal department, so that he would then ask his legal assistant, and then the director would pass her information on to you.'

I couldn't believe it and was getting quite frustrated. 'Look,' I said, 'I'm rushed off my feet like everyone else in this company. I'm not a channel for passing information. What do you think the company pays me for?' My Chinese employee clearly wasn't concerned about the most effective way to get this done. What counted for him was making sure that everyone's face was saved.

This stuff is hard to deal with. I'm under tremendous pressure to achieve the best results and my staff is more concerned with face-related rituals that we don't even understand."

It is often those differences in priorities that cause major problems between foreign entrepreneurs and their Chinese employees. There is a constant battle between saving face and being economical and it is the foreign boss's job to find a good balance and make it work.

The question is: which way should the boss go? Should he go for face or for efficiency? In other words, should he adopt the Chinese practices, or should the Chinese employee adapt to the foreign approach and learn to put face issues aside? There are many heated debates about this and opinions are varied. Ideally, face and economic imperatives should coincide in order to sustain the profitability of a company and respect and preserve its employees' culture and ritual needs. If only it were so easy.

Here are a number of quotes from people who have come across this dilemma and have formed their own opinion:

"When there's a problem it has to be solved. Full stop. Like it or lump it. I have economic targets and am therefore often forced to disregard face even if I know that in many cases I'm failing to respect the sacred code. For me economic problems are more important than problems of face. In Chinese culture the opposite is true: face is much more important than anything else. The Chinese would be ready to sacrifice their entire department over a single question of face."

(A French businessman who has been living in China for over 20 years and now runs his own company there).

"Some people seem to think that in times of globalization where we all melt together and try to work the same way, there is no need to worry about face anymore. In my view this is a mistake. Anyone who has decided not to change his attitude and to totally ignore problems of face will either not last very long in China or will encounter a great deal of problems with the Chinese. Whatever the foreign country you are being sent to, there are always cultural beliefs and practices to respect. It's all very well to try and do it the

European or American way, but we should never lose sight of the fact that in reality it is us who have come to China. This doesn't just go for business by the way, it also goes for things in your private life, such as food. Yes, we are used to and like to eat Western food, but the day-to-day cuisine here remains Chinese. You cannot expect the Chinese to change that."

(A European director of human resources who spent over seven years in China).

"The more we develop the economy, the more we need fast answers and to resolve problems rapidly. In that context, the over-importance assigned to face to the detriment of efficiency is bordering on the unacceptable here in China."

(A Chinese finance director).

"Face is important but you shouldn't be spending more time handling all these face-related issues than clearing the mountain of work piling up on your desk!"

(A Spanish businessman who spent six years in China).

"In my opinion, we should adjust our management style and our way of doing things. We should anticipate that everything will be a little less efficient in this country and just accept it. The key is to find a way of working together effectively while trying not to cause others to lose too much face along the way. In my view, it's certainly the most coherent attitude to deal with it since it combines the efficiency demanded by the market and the need to adjust to the differences in Chinese culture."

(An American manager who has been in China for ten years).

"What people sometimes forget is that we are all guests here. Believe me, we don't make the laws. My role is to help foreign companies and managers who decide to move to China to be as efficient as possible and to make money. If saving your Chinese business partners' face means accepting late deliveries which is bad for your business, granting an excessive loan which represents a major risk for the company or any other highly negative impact, my advice is to go ahead and let the Chinese lose face. However, if the impact

on your business is not particularly serious, I would advise you, in terms of efficiency, to handle the face with the greatest of care."
(A Chinese consultant).

If there is a real risk for the company, ignore face.

In Summary

To take the Chinese concept of face lightly under the pretext of efficiency can cause a whole series of losses: loss of contract, loss of personnel, loss of money. Then there are cases where we feel like we can afford to pay less attention (unqualified and easy-to-replace personnel, no contact with high-ranking Chinese, financial imperatives, etc.).

In China, the art lies somewhere in the middle. It lies in being able to combine efficiency and face, while staying true to yourself.

Chapter 1: Brainteaser—Test your knowledge

1. The Chinese:

    a.   constantly apologize.
    b.   constantly ask others to apologize.
    c.   prefer to apologize rather than to lose face.
    d.   prefer to lose face rather than apologize.
    e.   neither since apologizing means losing face.

Answer: b. and e. It is interesting to note that the Chinese demand formal apologies from those who have caused them to lose face, but are reluctant to apologize themselves.

This extract from an article in *Le Figaro* entitled "Say Sorry or Lose Face" sums it up nicely: "Saying sorry in China equates to assuming responsibility for making a mistake. This in turn equates to losing face, which is the equivalent of social death. Simply saying "sorry" or "excuse me," which is so common in the Judeo-Christian tradition, is a traumatic experience in the Middle Empire."

2. Check the right answers:

Not taking face seriously when dealing with the Chinese can lead to:

    [ ]   loss of money.
    [ ]   loss of time.
    [ ]   reluctant staff.
    [ ]   an early departure from China.

Being obsessed with face when dealing with the Chinese can lead to:

    [ ]   loss of money.
    [ ]   loss of time.
    [ ]   anarchy among staff.
    [ ]   a heart attack.

Answer: Check all boxes.

3. What formula strikes you as being the most applicable in China?

a. Power beats law.
b. An iron fist in a velvet glove.

Answer:

—"An iron fist in a velvet glove" is the most effective attitude in China. It is all about paying attention to face while demonstrating firmness and authority.

—"Power beats law:" imposing your viewpoint and decision by force while refusing to respect your business partner's face does not work in China. A full-blown open conflict will only work for a short period of time or with lower-level employees.

Also, counting on the law and your rights in China to resolve conflicts is purely illusory. In China, it is not the law but face that determines people's behaviors. In the event of a dispute it is always better to focus on the questions of face and power struggles than taking matters before a court.

4. When you cause a Chinese to lose face, who else also loses face? :

a. His parents.
b. His great aunt.
c. Yourself.
d. Every citizen in the People's Republic of China.

Answer: All.

When a Chinese loses face, it is not only he who loses face but also his employees, his family and everyone he represents or to whom he is connected. This is likely to be a leftover from practices in ancient China where a sanction or disapproval from the Emperor over a member involved the entire clan. When an individual was condemned to death, sometimes the entire clan was put to the sword.

Similarly, he who causes someone to lose face, loses face himself. In China, causing a loss of face and losing face are two closely related notions. For instance, if you criticize your employee in public, you cause him to lose face, but you also lose face since such an attitude is not appropriate for a real leader who knows how to restrain himself and stay in control regardless of the circumstances. Conversely, if an employee criticizes his superior in public, he causes him to lose face but he also runs the risk of losing face by being fired.

5. Which of the following statements is true?

    a. A Chinese person would be prepared to resign if he could earn 100 Yuan (10 Euro/15 USD) more with another company.
    b. A Chinese person may resign if you cause him to lose face.
    c. You may end up resigning yourself due to all these questions of face stressing you out.

Answer: The Chinese do not hesitate to resign for simple questions of face, especially when the Chinese job market is booming. The salary can also be a reason for resignation, particularly among the younger generations. In the end, earning a lot of money is also a question of face.

The following chapters will help you to put these minor face-related problems into perspective.

Chapter 2

Respect the hierarchy

A Chinese man returns home unexpectedly and catches his wife in bed with another man. He is about to raise merry hell when he realizes that the man is no other than his own boss. Realizing this, he meekly makes up a bed on the sofa to make sure he does not wake him.

The next morning his boss says to him: "Good work comrade, I slept like a baby."

(Humorous illustration of the undying loyalty the Chinese are expected to show their bosses).

In China hierarchies dominate everyday life.

Anyone failing to grasp this is likely to cause a considerable loss of face amongst their Chinese relationships.

Not that the system of hierarchy would only be prevalent in China. In many cultures, criticizing a high-ranking person in a large assembly or bypassing him will surely offend him. But, in China, hierarchies are at the core of life. This is not a strictly professional phenomenon, but also found in families, social networks and any other environment that involves human interaction. Everywhere and at all levels of Chinese social life you will encounter a hierarchy with strict codes that everybody is expected to comply with.

Thus, what Europeans or Americans might merely observe in high-level or diplomatic negotiations in their country, would take place in any Chinese business—including in rundown Chinese factories producing slippers or rubber baskets in the middle of nowhere.

It was in a small Chinese barber shop that a European executive discovered the weight of Chinese hierarchy by unknowingly breaking the rules:

"One day my usual barber was busy with another customer. So I asked if someone else could cut my hair so I wouldn't have to wait too long. My Chinese wife (who is more clued up on these subtleties than I am) shot me a disapproving glance and whispered a warning in my ear: 'Don't you think it would be better to wait?' 'No,' I replied stubbornly. I noticed that my usual hairdresser looked a bit miffed to say the least. I remember being really worried about him and I said to my wife: 'He doesn't look very happy, honey, I wonder what's wrong with him. Maybe he's got personal problems?'

The next time I went to the shop, I walked up to the second hairdresser (who by the way had turned out to be much better at his job than my original stylist) and shook his hand. My usual barber became hysterical. My wife got very mad at me for that and said that it was all totally my fault.

From then on, my wife insisted on organizing my appointments personally. It soon dawned on me that she always chose Thursdays, the day that my original hairdresser was off. She was helping him to save face. In China, hierarchy exists even at the tiniest barber's shop. This hairdresser was the number one in the salon and therefore should be respected the most."

Hierarchy

Chinese society is based on a steep hierarchical system which originates from Confucianism. The system defines everyone's place in society and the relationships they must cultivate with others. There are reciprocal obligations: respect on one side and protection on the other. In the Chinese system there are five types of relationships that are of outmost importance. It fixes the five cardinal relations: the relationship between son and father, wife and husband, younger brother and older brother, subject and Emperor, and finally youngest friend and oldest friend.

All personal relationships are founded on the same basis, which themselves originate from the highly organized family structures.

In fact, this system is more than just a mere demonstration of respect for hierarchy; in the business world there is a notion of irrevocable loyalty which is reflected in the obligation to protect the face of managers and other high-ranking figures. The human resources director of a major French group is convinced that:
"A Chinese team would never gang up to get their manager fired, which is a sort of thing that can perfectly happen in France."

Food for thought:

A Chinese teacher: "Order and hierarchy reigns in society. A loss of face creates an obstruction and undermines this established order."

Chinese proverb: "The dragon that flies the highest will fall from the greatest height."

The Chinese never question their superiors

I had the following exchange of thoughts with a Chinese director who had spent several years in France:

Q: I asked you to talk about face and here you are talking about hierarchy.

A: Well, yes, precisely because face is above all a question of hierarchy. For instance, in China you are not allowed to contradict your superior, otherwise he will lose face.

Q: But it isn't exactly easy to get away with contradicting your boss in France either. Even if French people tend to challenge everything which resembles authority, we too have a highly hierarchical system. So what's the difference?

A: This is precisely it, you just said it yourself. In France, you challenge authority. In China, you cannot challenge your superior's authority under any circumstances. Picking on your boss's comments in front of other people causes a considerable loss of face. You cannot say the slightest thing to your superior which may undermine his credibility and, by extension, the credibility of the company. You would run the risk of unhinging the entire system.

In China, contradicting your boss is simply inconceivable.

Your boss can talk the worst kind of nonsense and nobody will dare to doubt his words. For example: if you are the boss, you can come back from a business trip to Brazil and announce cheerily to everyone in the office that there are eight times as many women in the country as men. Everyone will nod in agreement. The German who told this particular story could not stop himself from responding in front of his stunned Chinese colleagues: "Are you sure about that? Sounds like you spent most of your time in nightclubs! I doubt that this ratio is accurate in the real life."

A Spaniard who works for a French group in China says:

"In France, you can say to your boss: 'I don't agree with you.' Here in China nobody would dare tell me that I'm wrong! That doesn't mean that I'm always right or that I've suddenly become very clever since I moved to China. It just means that I'm the boss."

A French manager adds:

"It's funny because in France nobody agrees with you and in China, on the contrary, everyone agrees with you. I don't let myself be blinded by the Chinese way but I have to admit that it makes it a lot easier to take decisions."

So to those of you out there kidding yourselves—get ready to be disillusioned. Just because everyone agrees with you, you are not automatically right or have taken good decisions. Your employees simply acknowledge that you are the boss.

Although this fawning can sometimes be quite comfortable, the consequences can be serious if you are not paying attention enough. The following two people tell their story.

A Western doctor who lived in China for many years recalls this particular experience:

"I remember one day telling a group of medical students that I was training: 'In medicine, the only face that counts is that of the patient.' The reaction was icy to say the least. You could tell I'd said something I shouldn't have. I'd definitely hit a nerve.

In the area I work in, face is of enormous importance. I have to deal with it on a daily basis. Here's just one example: when I refer a patient to a radiologist for an x-ray and I write "suspected pneumonia" (which is the sort of thing I would do back then), you can be sure that my patient always received the confirmation that he suffered from pneumonia—simply because the radiologist wouldn't want to cause me to lose face by saying my diagnosis was wrong. These days, I make no mention of the symptoms so as not to influence his decision."

An American woman tells a story about her unfortunate British friend:

"At a major ceremony marking the authorization for the company to start trading in Beijing, my British friend wanted to offer a gift to each of the guests (over 100 people in total, including customers and members of the government). In the UK, it is common practice to give out, say, large golfing umbrellas bearing the company logo. He thought they would be the perfect gift. He went around several of his Chinese departments to discuss these umbrellas. First, he asked the accountants to approve the budget which they duly did. He then went to the purchasing department to instruct them to find somebody who could manufacture the right type of umbrella. So they found him a supplier. Finally, he brainstormed with his marketing staff on color and logo of the umbrellas.

On the day of the event, everything was ready for the big ceremony. But guess what? None of the guests actually ever received an umbrella.

What my British friend did not know was that in China umbrellas should never be given as gifts, especially not to celebrate the start of a new business venture. In fact the word for umbrella in Chinese, *san*, is pronounced identically to the word meaning "to separate."

Everyone went along in the preparations of the gifts knowing exactly that the umbrellas would never be given out. A lot of energy and money was wasted simply because the employees didn't want their British boss to lose face."

STOP *In China, the boss is always right—at least on the surface.*

Follow the pecking order

❖ **Principles of equality versus principles of hierarchy**

"I don't think I committed too many cultural mistakes in terms of hierarchy. However, I think a mistake I did make in the very beginning was to treat everybody the same way," admits this European director. "I was uncomfortable with the fact that my Chinese employees bent over backwards to treat me well just because I was in charge. I also hated the fact that they kept calling me "boss" and I had asked them so many times to call me by my first name—which most of them never did. I soon realized that it just doesn't work that way in China."

This somewhat informal and familiar way of dealing with employees which is natural to European or American business people, actually brings the Chinese into embarrassing situations. An American confirms this:

"In the United States and also in many European countries you have this strong idea of all men being equal. The Chinese do not value this and accept that not all men are equal. In China the principles of equality are powerless against the principles of hierarchy."

This does not mean, however, that people from different social "classes" do not mingle in China. It just means that relationships in China are strictly hierarchical in the world of business and it is therefore acceptable, and even expected, to cultivate "unequal" relationships with your employees.

This also extends to the private life of foreigners who live in China. A Chinese woman who manages an *ayi's* agency talks about the relationships between foreigners and their Chinese housekeepers:

"The problem with many foreigners is that they tend to address their *ayi* like a friend. Not only are the Chinese employees likely to be thrown off balance but they may confuse "camaraderie" with a "lax" attitude and take advantage of the situation. The pecking order must be perfectly clear from the start: I'm the boss, you're the employee. I respect you and you respect me. That doesn't mean that you shouldn't establish a friendly environment. On the contrary, the Chinese are very sensitive to that sort of thing. Most *ayis* prefer to be thought of as members of the family (where hierarchical structures are also prevalent) rather than a friend."

---

* The term *ayi* is used for housekeepers and means "aunt" in Chinese.

Do not confuse respect with fellowship.

❖ Draw the line according to hierarchy

"Where foreigners make the most mistakes, is when they don't consider it necessary to treat people according to their hierarchical levels and social status," explains a Chinese teacher who worked as an interpreter for numerous foreign delegations. "This is a big mistake. In China, if you treat the boss and his employees equally, the boss loses face. Respect does not only mean being nice to the managers but also acknowledging and paying attention to all of the little hierarchical rituals."

This aspect is illustrated by the everyday gesture of a regular handshake. Say a Chinese director just accompanied you back to your hotel. If you shake the director's hand and then his driver's, you will cause the director to lose face and make the driver feel ill at ease.

A Chinese would respect both individuals, but use different ways to address and acknowledge them. He may shake the director's hand and then bow his head to the driver to thank him for his services.

Respect and highlight hierarchical distinctions.

The most common mistakes

❖ Greeting managers

"Foreigners sometimes neglect details to which Chinese managers are particularly sensitive," explains the director of a Chinese business. "This is where they cause managers to lose face the most."

One of the examples he cites is the way of greeting a Chinese manager:

"When you receive a Chinese top executive, it is vital to welcome him with a sign indicating his name, post and company name to notify the staff of his imminent arrival and to organize a reception committee. If nobody is aware of his visit when he arrives and you are the only one there to greet him, the Chinese executive may suffer significant loss of face in the eyes of those accompanying him. This numbers game is extremely important in China and also applies to negotiations: if the Chinese turn up with five people then we will have to get together five of our people as well. It's all about balance. If there are only two of us, this suggests that they are not important enough and if there are ten of us, they may feel overpowered and vulnerable.

It is important to treat the manager as a VIP to underline his high status. It is also important to understand that by showing respect to the chief, his staff will feel respected. It is the entire organization represented by the chief which is valued."

Similarly it is important to receive the Chinese in your nicest lounge or conference room. Greeting someone in a sumptuous reception area means you have lots of face and give face to your visitors.

Invest in your reception areas and dedicate special attention to the highest ranking person in the group.

❖ The importance of titles

The Chinese attach high importance to names and titles. You will quickly realize that they never forget your name (something you may not be able to guarantee in return). A Chinese teacher tells how she suffered the worst possible loss of face when she forgot the name of a renowned professor she was meeting (her fall-back solution was to use the title of *laoshi* or "professor"). She felt she was a whisker away from causing the visiting academic considerable loss of face.

Not only is it important to remember the names of your business partners but also to use their titles. Calling a Chinese director *Wang jingli* (the name of the Wang family followed by the title of manager), or *Li Zongjingli* (managing director Li) is a way of emphasising his rank and giving him face. You should therefore make every effort to remember the titles of the people you work with, even if the Chinese will not get overly offended if you use "Mr." or "Mrs." instead.

Whatever you do, avoid calling them by their first names (unless the person in question is an old friend). In fact, the Chinese almost never use first names (apart from the English first names which a lot of Chinese people have adopted*). In general, you have to wait for the relationship to become pretty close before passing on to this stage. Even people who know each other well or old-time colleagues use *xiao* (little) followed by the surname, or the respectful *lao* (old or elderly) followed by the surname when talking to older people.

Address people using their title followed by their surname.

❖ The hierarchical path

In general, it is fairly easy for a foreigner to gain access to Chinese top management. However, what seems helpful at first glance can be quite risky in some cases.

After having worked in China for seven years, this European manager concludes:

---

*   The Chinese use English first names to facilitate communication with foreigners but also because it is fashionable. Even in Chinese firms, some find English more practical for signing E-mails. They may choose a standard first name such as *Joyce* or *James* . . . One got the name "Frog" from his English teacher. Another Chinese employee opted for the nickname of "Seven" simply because he liked drinking Seven Up.

"Failing to respect the hierarchical path and wanting to deal directly with the person at the top of the ladder is a mistake that a lot of foreigners make. Not only do we cause considerable loss of face in the process but this tactic often turns out to be ineffective. In many cases the boss will want to consult those beneath him before making a decision, and in any case most of the negotiations have to be conducted with the base (although there may be additional contact with the superiors on some occasions to support the project)."

A Chinese director sheds some light on this issue:

"There are two scenarios:

Scenario 1: if you don't know anyone in the company, it's a big mistake to attempt to gain direct access to the top person. Since he doesn't know you and therefore has not established a relationship of trust with you, he will most certainly tell you to follow protocol and refer you to another department. The manager of that department will then be furious at having received orders from high up, assuming that to you he is not a key contact since you didn't bother to consult him in the first place. He'll probably give you a hard time. So for initial contacts it is wise to start at the bottom.

Scenario 2: if you have already worked with the company and established close contacts with both ends of the corporate ladder, I would advise going straight to the top in order to gain some time and be more efficient. When the big boss has made his decision nobody will tamper with it."

Respect the hierarchical path and everyone will be on your side.

❖ Communication by "levels"

A Chinese may lose face if you send one of his compatriots of a lower hierarchical level to him to negotiate or submit a request.

"If I send an assistant to ask a director something I need to know, I not only run the risk of causing the director a considerable loss of face but also diminish every chance to get the desired response," explains this European HR director. "In Chinese business, communication happens only between people on the same level. Thus, a Chinese manager will meet another manager and the vice-president will only open his door to another vice-president. And if you want to meet the minister for industry, then you'll have to get at least your country's ambassador to accompany you."

This Norwegian woman still remembers the first time she was confronted with the notion of face in China:

"One day, my *ayi* asked my landlady's driver to come inside and help her fix a leak. A few days later, my landlady came to see me. I'd never seen her so angry: 'You should never have allowed the *ayi* to ask my driver directly, you should have asked him yourself!' She then gave my *ayi* a real tongue-lashing.

This was strange to me because the fact that my *ayi* didn't bother me for such a minor detail struck me as perfectly normal and even creditable. In Norway, we prefer it when people take initiative. In fact this is what we encourage our children to do from a very early age. But by taking initiative (in itself a rare event in China) the *ayi* had committed a serious cultural crime—especially since, as a Chinese national, she is expected to be familiar with the codes. Instead she had failed to respect the rules of hierarchy. The *ayi* is not important enough to give orders to a driver and this was not just any driver, it was my landlady's driver.

This is when I discovered that there were communication rules by "levels." This was all very strange to me, especially since in Norway, communication is always horizontal, even in companies."

This experience is easily transferable to the business context. Sending a fresh-faced young salesman to negotiate directly with a director, which often happens in Western countries, can cause a Chinese director to lose face. Even if some Chinese managers are getting used to being introduced to people who are much younger than they are and the foreign status somewhat minimizes the loss of face incurred, it remains true that if you want to have a fruitful business relationship you should send someone who has been around for a while and earned his stripes.

This Spanish company manager understands the importance of going to meetings personally:

> "I honestly couldn't count the number of times I've gone to meetings simply to "show my face" to get a contract signed, while back home I wouldn't need to be present."

You can also rally the ambassador or consul of your home country to the cause, as recommended by this Chinese director: "This will give a lot of face to your business partner and make business so much easier."

If the ambassador is unavailable either way, I suppose your own boss could go—it could be worth it.

Send an experienced or middle-aged salesperson and get the boss to show up when you are closing the deal.

❖ **Demonstrating self-esteem**

Some people think that to avoid causing the Chinese to lose face you need to demonstrate that they are much more important than you. This is not strictly true.

Although showing your business partners in front of others that they are prestigious persons will definitely give them face, presenting yourself as very inferior will cause them to lose face (see previous section). In fact, the more you present yourself as an eminent figure, the more face you will give your business partners. Be aware of the boundaries, though. Giving face is not about behaving in a superior or arrogant manner, but rather about sending out signals to show that you are an influential person.

A Chinese director who works with the French Chamber of Commerce says:

> "It is vital to value *yourself* in order to value others. If I introduce myself in a run-of-the-mill sort of way, I make my business partner feel like he is not particularly important. Foreigners don't always pay attention to this aspect, whereas the Chinese attach a great deal of importance to it. Having a driver, waiting for someone to open your door or sending someone to the reception to announce your arrival shows a certain standing. Everyone in the company will then know that your business partner is superior enough to receive an important person."

A Frenchman working in public relations gives another example:

> "When I try to promote our business school to Chinese students, I nonchalantly slide across my business card from Fudan University (a highly prestigious university in Shanghai). This gives me kudos in their eyes. You have to know how to exploit this. In sales, only two things count: what you say and what you represent. This latter aspect is crucial in China."

The Chinese are extremely sensitive to status symbols and signs of success. What would be criticized as showing off in certain countries is perfectly normal in Chinese communities.

The experience of this wealthy Chinese businessman who returned home from the US speaks volumes:

> "I spent 20 years in the United States. Over there everyone uses cabs, whether they're workers or businessmen. It's no big deal. I hadn't been back in China for very long when I decided to take a cab to get to a business meeting (as had been my custom in the States). Upon my arrival everyone was waiting for me at the entrance.
>
> When I got out of the cab I could already see the disappointment on their faces. The car I was getting out of simply did not match my supposed status in their eyes.
>
> I learned a lot from this experience. The car represents your position and the value of the company (is it a powerful company

with sound finances or a small firm with limited resources?). First impressions are crucial. People in China attach massive importance to what they see. Although I don't personally attach much importance to cars, I ended up buying one—a Ferrari.

From then on, I didn't have to fend off a bunch of questions anymore every time somebody was trying to establish my professional position or social status. The Ferrari definitely changed people's attitudes towards me. I get the red-carpet treatment wherever I go and can meet whomever I want to. Making business is so much easier now."

> **STOP** *To meet your Chinese contacts turn up in a chauffeur-driven Mercedes rather than a cab.*

This anecdote from an Italian marketing director is a nice way to conclude this chapter:

"I was sent to China to take up a post as head of marketing and to support an existing team which already had a Chinese marketing director. Although she held onto her title of "marketing director," as the new boss I took her seat in meetings with the other directors.

One day she asked if we could talk in private (I immediately feared the worst. I knew from experience that when a Chinese person wants to talk to you about something, you're usually in a crisis situation). She cornered me. 'Since I've stopped attending meetings, I no longer feel respected by you or the rest of the company. Either I get to participate in meetings again or I will resign.'

I was really shocked. I can fully understand why being left out of meetings can cause offense (whether you're Chinese or not), but I thought it would be more humiliating for her to sit in on the meetings without being able to give any input than not being there at all.

Since we wanted her to stay we decided to let her participate in meetings even though we knew it was a waste of her time and totally inefficient.

During the meetings she never said anything, but to her that's not what mattered. Her image in the company was at stake and that's what she was most concerned about. Even if none of the directors in the meeting was fooled by it, her face had been saved."

In Summary

If saving the face of Chinese employees is important, saving that of managers certainly should be an absolute priority.

Whatever you do, help them to keep their image safe.

Chapter 2: Brainteaser—Test your knowledge

Check the right answers.

1. To your Chinese employees you should be a:

    a. confidant.
    b. father figure.
    c. bully.

Answer: b.

In China the boss-employee relationship is similar to the father-son relationship. The boss must demonstrate authority and be protective towards his employees, who must in turn demonstrate respect and total confidence.

An Austrian woman employed as a director in China, makes the following comment:

"In China, I sometimes feel like I'm a real mother hen with my workers."

2. How do you spot someone who is high up in the organization?

[ ] He is seated in the center opposite the door during a banquet or near the person in the center opposite the door.
[ ] He speaks first at a banquet, begins to eat first ("moves his chopsticks" first—in Chinese: *dong kuai zi*), and leaves the table first.
[ ] He will not turn up at your event if you have failed to make arrangements for other big players to attend.
[ ] During negotiations he keeps his distance and only shows up at the end to sign the contract.
[ ] He talks to you about China and your home country. These are the main subjects you can discuss with him.

Answer:

Just check everything.

3. **For a Chinese manager, which of the following situations is not particularly serious in terms of face?**

   a. Losing his camera on a trip to Paris.
   b. Having a son who has only been accepted into Tongji University instead of Fudan University (the top two universities in Shanghai).
   c. Not having a secretary.
   d. Wearing the same suit as his workers.

   Answer: d.

   To the Chinese a car is more important in terms of face than clothing. A French manager observes: "In China, it's sometimes hard to tell the director apart from his workers (they're all wearing the same suit). You can only tell he's the director when you see him getting in or out of his big fancy car!"

   As for the camera, it's not losing it which causes a loss of face but losing what it contains. Although a trip to a foreign country generates a lot of face you still have to bring back the proof. A Chinese woman explains:

   "The Chinese take lots of photos so they can show them to friends. What will friends think if you don't produce the photos? That I didn't actually go on the trip. I went to Paris ten years ago but I still show the photos I took in front of the Eiffel Tower. In France people take photos mainly as souvenirs even though they sometimes like to share them with friends. In China, people mainly take photos for reasons of face."

4. **A Chinese man is faithful to:**

   a. his wife.
   b. his boss.
   c. his dog.

Answer:

I really could not comment on the extent to which Chinese men are devoted or faithful to their wives since I do not have any statistics to hand. Anyway, I prefer not to go down that path.

Talking about dogs, there are many regions in China where dog is not eaten, although dog stew is a Cantonese speciality and the Chinese are increasingly keeping them as pets. To such an extent that the city of Shanghai decided in 2011 to establish the "one dog policy" as a way of controlling the increasing dog population. But apart from making stews or loving them as pets, there is no particular reason why the Chinese would be faithful to our canine friends.

What is certain is that the Chinese are devoted to their bosses—both in terms of respect and the extent to which they will do everything to prevent them from losing face. But this kind of loyalty does not necessarily mean that they will never walk out on the company.

Chapter 3

Never criticize in public

> *When you hit someone,*
> *don't hit them in the face.*
> Chinese proverb

You probably know people who excel at the art of criticizing and embarrassing others in public. The Chinese consider this urge to speak one's mind a sign of ignorance towards other people's feelings. Not only does this behavior cause the Chinese to lose face but even more so it is considered ill-mannered. Such obvious lack of tact could only come from a *wai guo ren* (a foreigner).

Unless they are deliberately setting out to cause somebody to lose face, the Chinese will take great care not to criticize the comments or works of others in public.

A Western woman remembers somebody being dressed down in public by his foreign boss:

"At the time, I worked as a hotel trainee in China. During a meeting my German boss began shouting at the Chinese restaurant manager in front of his colleagues, and even worse, in front of his subordinates; all this just because of one customer complaint. After a real tongue-lashing during which the restaurant manager stayed tight-lipped (as did everyone else for that matter) I decided to step in: 'I was there when it happened. I think the customer was being unreasonable and had no cause to complain.'

This stopped my boss's tantrum and all he could say was 'Oh really?'

After this episode, the Chinese man in question thanked me profusely. I had no idea it was so important for him. I hadn't realized that my intervention saved his face. I just acted without thinking about it much. And I'm sure that if I'd set out to save his face by saying things like 'It's really not his fault' or 'He did nothing wrong' I would have made things worse since the others would have judged him and assumed he was incapable of defending himself.

After this incident a basket of fruit was left in my room at the start of every week (a treatment normally reserved for VIPs) and I received many other favors of this kind while I lived and worked at the hotel. And whenever I asked the restaurant manager for something I was always given priority."

The culture of harmony

Confucianism favors harmony between individuals and considers it the source of equilibrium in the universe and happiness for all creatures. Protecting each other's face means that harmony, or at least the appearance of harmony, is being preserved. This explains why the Chinese tend to avoid sources of conflict (criticizm, direct confrontation, the expressions of anger, etc.) at any price. Looking at it from this perspective it seems to be better to deal with problems internally, away from prying eyes, thus avoiding loss of face and ensuring harmony.

On the other hand, for Europeans and Americans, confrontation is not necessarily a bad thing. It is often even considered to be an effective way of resolving problems. Collective harmony contrasts with the notion of individual freedom and the right to say what you think. From this point of view, it is important to expose problems in order to resolve them even if it means identifying a guilty party.

Example:

China was hit by SARS (Severe Acute Respiratory Syndrome) in 2003. At first the Chinese people knew nothing about the dangerous epidemic; harmony prevailed, and face was preserved. European and American media agencies increased their coverage of SARS through various media channels to force the Chinese government to publicly address the issue and find a solution. Apart from the panic that spread amongst the Chinese population, this coverage also caused China (as the designated guilty party) to lose considerable face.

Avoid pinpointing the guilty party and keep internal problems inside: this is the rule of harmony and face.

Three basic rules

❖ No public, no face

Face can only be lost in a public situation. In other words, you always lose face if a third party is watching.

This is a key point.

"When they're at home spouses can argue as much as they like, that's not a problem," explains a Chinese man. "Face doesn't play a role in this. However, criticizing your spouse in front of others can be serious grounds for divorce in China."

For example, a Chinese husband would not dare criticize his wife's cooking in front of guests (which sadly is not always the case with Western husbands!).

Face is how others see you. This has not as much to do with any notions of personal guilt or intrinsic dignity. For instance, if someone commits a bad act but none witnesses it, there is no loss of face. However, they risk losing face if someone else is in the know. Similarly, if you criticize someone in private, they may be personally upset, but at least they won't have lost face in front of others.

In Chinese companies, you will rarely see a Chinese manager criticize one of his employees in public, something that is not uncommon in European companies, as this French director quite rightly points out: "In my country people don't hold back, but criticize pretty much on all corporate levels. Whereas, after five years spent in China, I've never seen one of my Chinese team members do that. They would never tell off a member of their team in the presence of others."

Hence you will not hear a Chinese person contradict a colleague in the middle of a business meeting, as this Chinese businessman explains:

"In a meeting with a Chinese client, a foreigner wouldn't think twice about cutting off a Chinese colleague by saying 'no, no, you're wrong, what you're saying is simply incorrect.' In China it doesn't work that way. Not only does the colleague lose face but it will also become very difficult to develop a good relationship with this client, who will obviously have difficulties trusting him after such a comment.

If a colleague questions your word and does not respect you it means that you are considered to be of low rank.

A Chinese would have probably discussed the colleague's statement over lunch in order to make necessary adjustments. However, he would have never brought it up during the negotiations and certainly not in front of the client."

So even if you are not bothered by whether or not other people are listening, know that to a Chinese this is of outmost significance.

Never criticize in public, but wait for a private moment.

❖ **The significance of a loss of face depends on the status of those who witness it**

In China, if someone is being criticized in front of a colleague of the same hierarchical level, he loses face. If he is being criticized in front of a subordinate or in the presence of people of a lower social position, however, he loses face twice as badly.

A Chinese plant director confirms this:

"When we are in an executive committee meeting attended by departmental directors we do argue; It isn't such an issue. However, if I were to criticize a departmental director in front of his employees it'd be a disaster! I sometimes tell off directors but never in front of their subordinates. On the other hand, my foreign boss quite happily criticizes my results in the company magazine, which of course is read by my lower-ranking financial controller and I hate that!"

I posed the following question to both Chinese and foreigners:

"What do you think is more humiliating: being criticized in front of your superior or being criticized in front of an employee?"

Their answers varied significantly. While the majority of foreigners replied "in front of my boss of course," the Chinese predominantly picked the second scenario. Here some of the responses:

"Without a doubt it's more serious in front of an employee. The worst is when it's in front of your inferiors."

"For me, it's worse to lose face in front of a domestic employee or a worker than in front of a superior."

"Never critisize in front of inferiors. In any case never in public, regardless whether in front of someone of higher or lower standing."

However, this Chinese manager gives some nuances:

"The Chinese never criticize anyone in front of their subordinates. If a client (who is the person most likely to do so) should ever criticize someone in front of their teams he's taking an enormous risk, since the others will systematically defend their boss (the clan-based society). On the other hand, he wouldn't hesitate to criticize someone in front of their superior in order to obtain something. If a client feels like criticizing me in front of my superiors it is much worse for me since I have more to lose than if it happens in front of employees who will support me."

Never criticize a senior person in front of his employees. Besides, you risk that they will all turn against you.

❖ The art of criticizing in China

"If you hit someone, don't hit them in the face," says the Chinese proverb. In other words, if you feel the need to criticize somebody, do so, but in a way that will allow the other person to make a good impression.

This is how an American, a French and a Chinese woman worded their criticizms when letting their cleaning ladies go (these examples are drawn from actual cases):

The American lady prepared a long list of everything she was unhappy with: "You don't clean behind the furniture, you never wash the pots and pans properly, you don't iron the shirts the way you should, etc."

The French woman was unsure of how to go about the whole thing. She felt bad and guilty for a month before she finally lost it. "This can't continue! You are doing a terrible job and I'm not satisfied at all!"

The Chinese woman said with a sympathetic smile: "Thanks for working for me, but I'm looking for someone who can speak English to my kids." She gives her maid the chance to leave with her head held high, using an honorable excuse. Even though the maid knows exactly why she has been fired, face is duly saved.

What can we learn from these experiences?

To begin with, we learn that it is best not to criticize in the heat of the moment. More even than the criticizm, it's often the fact of shouting that alert everybody around that causes the loss of face.

This Italian learned to hold back:

"In the Italian company I work for, everybody shouts all the time. That's the way we Italians are. I realized that I had to get rid of this behavior here when several Chinese women in my team broke down in tears when I criticized their work. Since then I've tried to tell them uncomfortable things in private (although this is not always possible when time is a factor) and use a more conciliatory tone. That seems to work because they pretty much stopped crying in my presence."

Also, have you ever noticed that the Chinese always smile when they have something unpleasant to tell you? So instead of losing patience, try to be cordial and do it Chinese style: smile!

A foreign manager noticed how effective this approach can be:

"When I have something harsh to say to my Chinese employees, I do so with a smile and a sense of humor. I noticed that this works much better, but at the same time it allows me to say what I have to say."

Finally, try to drop the personal pronoun "you" from your vocabulary.

"In foreign companies, criticizm often seem agressive," says a Chinese employee. "I think foreigners have a tendency to point their finger at people and say: 'That's not good enough. What have you done?' This is where they cause a loss of face the most. When there is a problem or when they want to express their criticizm the Chinese never mention the name of the person in question. Instead they talk about the particular case."

It is in fact possible to get your message across and save the other person's face at the same time. Put differently, you do not need to mention the person's name to make sure that your message hits home.

A consultant of Chinese origin often cites this ancient anecdote to his foreign clients:

"One day a servant stole some salt (a very expensive commodity at the time) from his master's cellar. The master found out but decided not to fire the man since he had been a faithful servant for many years. So he simply said: 'Someone stole the salt. Can you buy a new padlock for the cellar door? That way the thief won't be able to steal anymore.'"

The consultant concludes:

"The problem was solved and the master had saved his servant's face. This way of doing things is very Chinese.

Foreigners have an annoying tendency to try and identify the guilty party. They want to know who is responsible, so they spend more time on this aspect than resolving the problem itself. I have seen so many Americans, French, British and Germans accuse someone by saying 'It's your fault; you didn't do such and such; you this, you that.' It shouldn't be so much about identifying who is at fault but rather about resolving the problem in an effective manner."

Avoid pointing out who is guilty and concentrate on solving the problem.

Why even the Chinese sometimes criticize in public

We have seen that the Chinese go to extraordinary lengths to avoid criticizing the others in order to save their face. But that does not necessarily mean that they will never do it. It does not happen often but when it does, things can get heated.

❖ Making an example of somebody

Although the Chinese seem very attentive to the face of others, paradoxically they are also experts in public humiliation. Moreover, it is worth remembering that during the Cultural Revolution, being "criticized" clearly meant being humiliated in public.

The Chinese authorities regularly use public criticizm for dissuasive purposes. In Shanghai for example, they launched a campaign aimed at dissuading pedestrians from jaywalking or crossing a red light. The authorities had pictures taken of the citizens' illicit acts and then displayed them on public notice boards. A Chinese woman even resigned because she could not bear the loss of face caused at work when her colleagues spotted her picture.

Yet the Chinese managers interviewed for this guide said they rarely use these methods: "It's never a good idea to criticize someone in public, even if the criticizm is justified and you want others to learn from it."

Avoid public criticizm even if you are trying to make an example. Leave the police handle it.

❖ Firing somebody

In Chinese companies, public criticizm is commonly used to fire people. If you see a Chinese director criticizing someone in front of others, you can be pretty sure that their days with the company are numbered.

"One day a European director criticized one of his employees in front of the entire company. Like me, all the Chinese thought he was on his way out. This is what the employee thought, too and he preferred resigning. The director told me later that he had absolutely no intention of firing that guy. He even thought that he was a good employee and planned to keep him on the company's books well into the future."

If you strongly criticize an employee in public everyone will think you want to fire him.

❖ Defending your own face

A Frenchman tells this story:

"Our top executives recently came over from France to visit us in Shanghai. I sent the supplier to pick them up at the hotel. You can picture the scene: big bosses, luxury hotel, black Mercedes with chauffeur. So these French businessmen were comfortably installed in the back seat when the car pulled out of the parking space. After a couple of minutes the driver turned red with rage, slammed on the brakes, got out of the car and grabbed some guy who was walking down the street. After the driver had punched the hell out of him he calmly got back into the car and drove on as if nothing had happened. You can imagine the expressions on the faces of the French executives who couldn't figure out what was going on. The chauffeur later explained that this man had sold him something which didn't work. Whatever the reason, this simply showed us that the Chinese can lose their cool too!"

So yes, the Chinese can lose their tempers, too. Let's get rid of the cliché of Chinese who are imperturbable and spend all their spare time doing tai chi.

A foreign executive says: "The Chinese are very calm people, they rarely show their emotions. However, they may throw themselves into a terrible rage, only to be able to demonstrate that they are saving their face."

So do not be surprised if you see Chinese people insulting each other in the Streets:

"In two years in China, I've seen more people arguing and fighting in public than I have seen in my entire life in France."

"In the United States, we often publicly criticize someone's work, it's not a problem. However, we don't throw public tantrums like the Chinese sometimes do."

Numerous conflicts come up every day in the streets of China over simple questions of face. To save face, in particular that of the family, some Chinese go to even greater lengths. An expatriate tells how his driver's wife had found herself in hospital with serious burns. One day, the driver's son (aged 6) had hit a neighbor's daughter. To save the family's face, the mother and grandparents of the girl in question had marched over to the driver's house where they beat his wife and threw a pot of boiling water over her.

Of course this is an extreme case and the vast majority of Chinese people, will resort to less violent means to save face. One very common option, for example, is to shout louder than your counterpart. A Chinese man explains:

"If I get criticized in front of everyone, the most direct way of saving face is to counterattack. I'll yell 'I totally disagree, this is all complete nonsense!' It will automatically lead to a conflict and a massive row. It's either me or him who loses face. That's the right of the strongest."

If a Chinese suddenly starts shouting at you, it may be because you unintentionally caused him to lose face.

Comments that irritate most foreigners

The Chinese sometimes have a way of blurting out the most unexpected things which often seem out of place in a society ruled by the notion of face. Some of those comments tend to shock and eventually annoy most foreigners.

Examples:

- A Chinese may say the following without so much as batting an eyelash: "You're looking old these days," or "Is this your new baby? He looks like he's got a malformation; he's so ugly!"
- Your former Chinese business partner whom you have not seen in months (and with whom you remain on friendly but professional terms) may tell you "Hey, you've really put on weight!" even before saying so much as "Hello."
- A Chinese woman is capable of nonchalantly telling her foreign fiancé: "Let's get married. That way I'll get the visa and in return

I promise I'll stay with you for at least 5 years." This flabbergasted the fiancé. He simply couldn't believe his ears. (Note: there are of course plenty of multi-national couples who are together for reasons other than visa regulations).

- If you tell a Chinese how much you paid for something, you will probably be told: "You paid way too much!" This comment immediately highlights your poor negotiation skills or even your stupidity for having paid three times more than a Chinese would have.
- You will be equally astonished by the matter-of-fact way with which a Chinese will tell you that your new jumper looks hideous on you.

However, if any of this happens, do not be offended. All of these somewhat clumsy comments are often the Chinese way of trying to be nice. As this middle-aged Chinese tries to explain:

"It's true that you can frequently hear comments such as: 'Your new hair style is a bit funny' or 'I don't like your new dress.' But it's not a criticizm. It's a bit like the expression *ni pang le* (you've put on weight), it's just a way of getting closer to the other person and showing you care about them.

In fact, the expression *ni pang le* is often used as a means to start a conversation (a bit like *ni chi fan le ma*? which literally means "Have you eaten yet?" and corresponds to "How are you?"). This might even be seen as a compliment, because the Chinese assume that if you are a bit on the chubby side, life is treating you well. It is often seen as a sign of good health and wealth, especially for people of my generation."

So really it is up to you to judge whether somebody is complimenting you, or really telling you to keep an eye on your weight.

If a Chinese makes a comment that seems very personal or direct, take it either as a compliment or a heartfelt piece of advice.

In Summary

In China people do not criticize in public, let alone in front of inferiors. If you do not want to risk losing your staff, respect this ground rule as much as possible. Avoid pointing out the guilty party and, above all, try to stay calm.

And if you witness a Chinese yelling at someone in public, then rest assured that it is a calculated attempt to make him lose face.

Chapter 3: Brainteaser—Test your knowledge

Check the right answers.

1. **In your view:**

   a. The Chinese never criticize in public.
   b. The Chinese always criticize in public.

   Answer:
   Both answers are wrong.

2. **Which of these two statements strikes you as correct?**

   a. The French hate being criticized in public.
   b. The Chinese hate being criticized in public.

   Answer: Neither the Chinese nor the French like to be criticized in public (nor any other nationality for that matter).

   A Chinese working in a French company makes the following comment:

   > "Many people say that the Chinese react badly to criticizm. This may be true, but I think they take it better than the French. At least the Chinese tend to not talk back, especially when the criticizm is coming from their managers. The French don't like being criticized but they sure love to dish it out!"

3. **In China, you can criticize another person:**

   a. if it's your spouse.
   b. if you are a teacher.
   c. if you are a police officer.
   d. if he is a police officer.

   Answer: All the answers are correct with a few adjustments:

   a. You can criticize your spouse, but only in private.

b. A Chinese saying goes: "Raising a child without educating him is the fault of the father, while educating a child without being strict is attributed to the schoolmaster's laziness." In Chinese schools, it is common practice for teachers to criticize pupils. Just like a father, the teacher fulfils an important educational role.

c. and d. Although the Chinese know it is in their best interest to respect the police, it is always amazing to foreigners to see how some of them behave towards the police. In fact, it is not unusual for a driver who has been pulled over for speeding to start arguing in order to defend his position and negotiate the fine. Usually a crowd gathers and people start giving their personal opinions: "You're totally right, the policeman has got it all wrong." "No, you're wrong, the policeman is right." However, if you have the impression that some Chinese people yell at police officers, it is simply because they try to speak a little louder than their counterparts (as a number of Chinese interviewees pointed out).

4. **In China throwing a tantrum equates to:**

a. being bad mannered.
b. demonstrating your power and earning respect.
c. showing that you cannot control yourself, which is a weakness.

Answer: a. and c.

When you get angry, not only do you risk coming across as ill-mannered, but also as someone who is weak.

A Chinese saying goes: "He who does not know how to anger is a fool, he who refuses to anger is a wise man." In other words, you have to know how to do it, but not do it. In business, a true manager therefore demonstrates his capacity to get angry while showing a tremendous amount of self-control.

5. **If a Chinese person criticizes you:**

a. It is for your own good.
b. He just wants to upset you.
c. It would not happen since you are the boss.

Answer:

Confucius said: "Those you love you should not spare hard labor. Those you respect you should not spare hard words."

When a Chinese person criticizes you it is often for your own good. (Unless they criticize you severely in public, which means they really want you to lose face). In the end, the Chinese never criticize you if you are the boss—at least not in public.

Chapter 4

The truth and nothing but the truth

If it doesn't need saying, don't say it.
Chinese proverb

Did you ever get the feeling in China that the person you are talking to is not telling the truth or is desperately trying to hide something? Do you remember how you felt? If there is one thing foreigners find hard to accept in China, it is that the Chinese tend to present the facts to their own advantage—often because of face-related issues that we fail to recognize.

To make things even more complicated, the version of the story told can change from one day to the next: not surprising in a culture of perpetual change where nothing is set in stone. This naturally collides with the idea of consistency that is prevalent in most Western countries where everything must be precise and established once and for all.

To Europeans and North Americans, nothing is more important than the truth. In fact, the latter base their entire political and social systems on this. The Chinese perspective is very different: saving one's own or someone else's face is often given priority over establishing any kind of truth.

The experience of this French businessman perfectly illustrates this:

"I made a major diplomatic mistake a few years back.

At the time I was selling machines that checked the thickness of roads (which must be of a certain depth to be considered of good quality). To convince the potential customer of my machine's effectiveness, I gave a demonstration and it turned out that the road I tested was not of the required thickness.

So during the meeting, I was extremely proud to present the results of the test demonstrating the capabilities of my equipment. I honestly thought the sale was as good as closed.

One of the Chinese observers then said to me: 'No, no, your machine doesn't work.' I was really surprised: 'Yes it does, I promise you.' Another Chinese chipped in: 'No, no, the road tested was of the right standard.'

I was determined to show them that my machine worked. It was out of the question that anyone could maintain the opposite which was untrue: 'Check with your own manual measuring system if you like, you'll see that this road is not compliant with the standards.'

For some strange reason their measuring system wasn't available at the time. The meeting was closed and the sale never happened.

Around the same period Jacques Chirac, President of France at the time, visited Beijing with a group of businessmen. I was having dinner with some VIPs and took the opportunity to share my strange experience with Jiang Zemin, who was serving the Chinese president. He replied: 'We need companies like yours and I'm calling on all of the senior people around the table today to contact you as soon as possible.'

When I got back to France all my efforts to follow up on the contacts failed."

The French businessman in question stubbornly insisted upon the fact that he was right and the Chinese were wrong, instead of recognizing that face was at stake. He would have done better had he not tried to vehemently make his point. Also it is entirely possible that other experts (perhaps even those present at the meeting) had already checked the road and they now would have been forced to admit that they had not done their job properly.

If he had paid more attention to face and less attention to establishing the truth, he would have had every chance to establish good business relationships with the Chinese.

The concept of truth

Westerners attach high importance to the concept of truth which mainly derives from their Judaeo-Christian culture and Greek philosophical tradition. The Bible is full with references to being truthful and "thou shalt not bear false witness" even made it into the Ten Commandments. Equally, one of the central premises of Greek philosophy is to seek the truth.

The Chinese have no notion of sin, which does not mean that they have no moral framework, but their moral values are part of a social order in which the notion of face plays a major part. Personal guilt then, is replaced by the notion of social shame.

In addition, the Chinese have never sought to accede to the truth, which they believe cannot be obtained since it is multifaceted and constantly shifting.

What must be either black or white in the Western mindset, can be grey to the Chinese. After all, their way of thinking is based on Yin and Yang, where nothing is ever firmly established—nothing is really totally black or white. To the Chinese a whole range of other possibilities and colors exists in between the two extremes.

Example:
Why are bridges in Chinese gardens zigzag shaped (an example cited by André Chieng during a lecture organized by the Alliance Française in Shanghai)?:

Chinese bridges are zigzagged to prevent ghosts (who—as everybody knows—only move in straight lines) from crossing them. Most of the time visitors are happy with this somewhat quaint response and accept it as the truth. And since there is only one truth other explanations cannot exist. However, a ghost that is unable to move forward in zigzags is neither very smart nor a very dangerous creature.

André Chieng raised this subject with a Chinese architect and asked him what he thought the truth was. The architect gave the following explanation: "The Chinese garden is a reduced representation of the world. It must display all of its diversity. If the bridges were straight, you would only get one perspective, whereas a zigzag bridge offers several."

Notice that the architect never said that the idea of the ghost was stupid but instead he added: "Mind you, that's my version, but there are plenty more out there."

So where does the truth lie?

Hiding mistakes

❖ To the Chinese revealing mistakes is a shameful act

A French company manager who has been living in China for over 20 years explains:

> "In Europe or America, lying is a source of shame. In China, making a mistake is a source of shame. I sometimes stubbornly try to prove that I'm right, but if it turns out that I'm wrong, I can admit my error and say 'Sorry, I was wrong' and then we get on with something else.
>
> However, a Chinese manager would never do or say something like that—after all his face depends on it."

This explains why a Chinese will refuse to budge from his position even when he has been proven wrong.

An American sales manager tells her story:

> "My Chinese legal advisor told me that the transaction we were working on at the time was perfectly legal. Effectively she was giving me thumbs up to close the deal. A few days later she suddenly changed her mind and said the exact opposite. I was confused but she insisted she had never thought otherwise.
>
> —I never said anything else, she maintained.
>
> —Yes you did.
>
> —It must have been another deal, she replied.
>
> I tried to put her at ease, because I thought perhaps the transaction had been legal before but it was no longer the case, as that can sometimes happen here. So I asked:

—Maybe the law has changed?

—No, it hasn't.

That's where I began to lose my cool:

—So why did you say one thing before and are now insisting on something completely different?

She refused to back down despite me demonstrating that I knew exactly that she had previously cleared the procedure.

She could simply have said 'Sorry, I was wrong,' and I'd have understood, but her reaction left me with the impression that she wasn't taking me seriously!

Even after having been in China for 10 years this is something I find hard to accept."

In Europe or the United States you will never see someone dig in their heels claiming they have not done something when all the evidence points to the contrary. But in China, this happens all the time.

"In the UK, if someone lies to you and others realize it's a lie then the person in question looks a fool. In China, you're the one who ends up looking foolish," complains a British executive.

John L. Chan touches on this aspect in his book "China Streetsmart:"

"What drives a lot of foreigners crazy is the fact that most local Chinese will never admit they are wrong. Even when the 'correct answer' is staring them in the face, they will never admit they are wrong. Actually, foreigners who feel this way are not acknowledging the cultural sensitivity of "losing face" in China. Furthermore, the local Chinese might genuinely not think they are wrong, given a difference in understanding and viewpoints."

When I had the opportunity to meet John L.Chan in Shanghai I asked him to elaborate:

"The problem with foreigners is that they start insisting: 'You told me it was blue and now you're refusing to acknowledge it's blue' or 'Come on, you can clearly see that it's blue!' This type of situation bears a lot of conflict."

Therefore, you have two choices: either you choose not to insist even if you are not taken in (which is what the Chinese will do most of the time), or you insist on making your Chinese counterpart admit that he or she made a mistake. Just be aware that they will then hide behind increasingly ludicrous explanations. You will most likely end up being exasperated, while making every effort to demonstrate that they are not being truthful. In the end, you will only waste your time and lose your temper. What's more, you will have caused them to lose face.

> *Do not bother trying to demonstrate that somebody made a mistake. Unless you have <u>irrefutable</u> proof and see no other way out, it really isn't worth the effort.*

❖ Nothing is ever a problem (*mei wenti*)

I raised the question of lies and truth with the father of a Chinese teenager, asking him what he taught his son:

> "Of course we also teach our kids not to lie, but I always tell my son: 'When you have good news, you must always tell us, but when it's bad, say nothing.' I recently had my wallet stolen with 50 yuans in it and my wife asked me what happened to the money. I told her that I had gone out for lunch with some friends. To avoid pointless problems you have to lie sometimes—that's the way it is. You've got to make sure harmony is being preserved."

This is something every visitor learns pretty quickly in China: the Chinese have a tendency to pass on the good news and hide the bad.

Mei wenti, in other words "no problem," is undoubtedly the expression you will hear most often in China. Note that *mei wenti* literally means "no question," in other words "I have no question to ask" (which of course does not necessarily mean that there is no problem).

You ask for a non-smoking room at the hotel reception. Seeing the puzzled expression on the receptionist's face, you begin to think your request may pose a problem. *Mei wenti!* The porter takes you up to a room that reeks of tobacco. You are about to complain when a maid marches in, removes an ashtray full of cigarette stubs, opens the windows, and starts spraying rose-scented air freshener. You now find yourself in a room smelling of roses and stale tobacco but what are you complaining about? You have got a "non-smoking" room.

What might seem like a scene from a hidden camera reality show is a situation encountered by a European businessman in Canton.

Later, you go down to the bar. You ask the barman for a chilled beer straight from the fridge. After several years in China you're still not used to drinking hot water (like Chinese do) and, even less, beer at ambient temperature, especially when it is 40°C/104° FT outside. *Mei wenti!* The barman grabs a six-pack of (warm) beer, shoves it in the fridge and immediately breaks one off the pack to serve you. So there you have it: "a beer straight from the fridge."

Is the barman or receptionist making fun of you? Or are they simply acceding to your request while concealing their inability to meet it? Or perhaps you simply didn't understand each other? It's a simple question of point of view.

But although a warm beer, or a "smoking, non-smoking room," gives you a funny story to tell, you definitely will not find it amusing when your employees reply *mei wenti* (no problem) when it is clearly a case of *you wenti* (there is a problem).

A foreign sales director remembers his first exchanges with a member of his sales team:

"1ˢᵗ quarter:
　　—How are things going with this client? Do you think you'll be able to meet the budget?
　　—*Mei wenti,* answered the salesman with such confidence that it was hard not to believe him.

2nd quarter:
   —Sales are poor. I'm worried.
   —*Mei wenti*, don't worry.
3rd quarter:
   By that time I understood where things were heading. I asked him specifically what he planned to do to catch up on the budget."

Always remember that your staff will have a tendency to "forget" to talk to you about problems, particularly when those problems are serious. A human resources director working for a major multinational offers some insight:

"In the Chinese plants we took over it was common practice that if a worker was the victim of an industrial accident, they were automatically disqualified from receiving a bonus. The result was that most accidents were not reported. We would sometimes only find out about them months later through workplace gossip. We got rid of this procedure and made it clear to the workers that they should keep us informed when an accident occurred rather than hiding it as they used to.

I keep telling my employees: 'Let me know if there's a problem, even if you've made a mistake. It doesn't matter. It's worse for me if you don't say anything.'"

If you feel that there is a problem, do not just accept mei wenti as an answer.

Leaving a way out

A Chinese company manager explains:

"Generally speaking, the Chinese will not admit that they have lied but will instead fall back on something like 'we must have misunderstood each other.' The wording will always contain a degree of ambiguity to leave room for maneuver.

Although the Chinese have a tendency to sidestep the issue, this is to ensure that there's always a way out (both for you and for them), in other words, a way of protecting everybody's face. That's why negotiating a contract can take an eternity!"

On this subject, a European human resources director remembers a commercial agreement signed between Europe and China in the 1980s, which until today puts a big smile on her face:

"You could actually see the many hours spent negotiating just by looking at the way the final document was worded. The Chinese always left windows open with formulations such as 'in the event of a divergence of opinion, an amicable solution should be found,' while the Europeans wanted unambiguous formulations like 'if no solution is found then restrictive measures must be determined' (which then of course were listed in detail).

For questions of face, the Chinese will always leave doors open to make sure everyone can retreat from what has been said without losing face."

While Europeans and Americans seek a definitive truth, the Chinese seek flexibility. We expect clear and straight-forward answers which the Chinese can rarely offer.

❖ **"Yes" or "no"**

The Chinese are often not prepared to give you a straight "no" because they are trying to avoid causing either of you to lose face. Similarly, they will avoid committing to a firm "yes" (because it would leave no room for maneuver in case they should change their mind). And if you get the feeling that they always say "yes," it is because they are simply incapable of saying "no" to you. Even more so, their "yes" does not necessarily mean your "yes." It is often closer to the "yeah, yeah" a child will throw at you when you ask him if he tidied up his room.

A Chinese man explains this further:

"If you ask a Chinese 'Can you do it tomorrow?' they will immediately think: if you ask this question you probably really need it done. Although I've got another obligation I can't say 'no.' That would be rude. So I discuss it and try to negotiate it. And in negotiations you can't start with a 'no.' I don't want to upset you, so I hesitate for a moment and then start with 'It's a bit difficult, but . . .' This is the Chinese way of going about such a problem."

A Chinese would have immediately understood the message while foreigners will keep insisting. This usually leads to lengthy and unnecessary discussions, until the foreigner will realize that the Chinese was saying "no" from the very beginning. Instead of saying no from the get go, the Chinese will come up with a number of different ways of expressing it to avoid sounding too direct. Moreover, the Chinese are often taken aback and sometimes even offended by the categorical "no" used by foreigners.

This account is from a French HR director:

"One day I turned down a request from a Chinese manager with a firm 'no' in the middle of a meeting (he was sure I'd said 'yes'). If we'd been alone in my office, face wouldn't have come into it, but in front of other people I really made him lose face. It took us a long time to get our relationship back on track after this incident."

A French entrepreneur shares his view:

"In China, people always try to reach a consensus by leaving room for maneuver. In France on the other hand people enter into conflict straight away before even thinking about reaching an agreement.
    Previously, when someone asked me for a pay raise, I would respond the French way—with a straight-forward 'no.' Now I do it the Chinese way and say, 'I will consider it,' so everybody is happy!"

If a Chinese employee asks you for a pay raise do not say "no" straight away. Instead say, "I will consider it."

❖ Linguistic ambiguities

Seemingly endless negotiations are not only a product of face-related issues but often also due to the inherent ambiguity of the Chinese language.

"The Chinese language allows for the construction of words or sentences with multiple meanings. A side effect is that you can always backtrack by saying, 'no, no, that's not what I actually meant,'" explains a Chinese director.

The nature of the Chinese language contributes strongly to the equivocal way of communicating in China. In Chinese, the same sound can have different meanings. For instance, the spoken word *bing* means "ice," "soldier," "cake," "sick," "stem," "presenting a report to a superior," "holding something in your hand," and "combine." Only the written word allows for precise differentiation.

Usually, the context of a word helps you to recognize its meaning and there are also certain tones (four to be precise) to tell similar words apart. Interestingly, even the Chinese sometimes have trouble telling the difference between similar words in conversations. Consequently, they are sometimes required to write out the ideogram or explain which *bing* they are talking about (hence the lengthy explanations when sometimes one sentence would do the trick in English).

Bing using the first tone means "ice," but since the "b" sound is like a "p" (at least to a foreigner) it is easy to confuse *bing* with *ping,* which means "bottle" in the second tone. If you ask for a bottle of water saying *ping shui* in a restaurant, you could end up with a *bing shui* (iced water), which in most cases is a jug of water boiled and then cooled down using ice cubes. By the way, you can circumvent this confusion by ordering bottled water by its brand name.

Also, in Chinese language even one single character can have several meanings. This is the case of the 送 character, pronounced *song* in the fourth tone:

"An estate agency runs a special offer to sell houses: '*mai fang zi, song jia ju*' 买 房 子 送 家 具. A Chinese man reads 'buy a house and get the furniture free' on the sign. Having just bought a house from them, he asks the estate agent when he can choose the free furniture. The agent replies: '*ni de jia ju zai nali? women bang ni song*' (Where is your furniture? We will help deliver it to your home).

In fact, *song* 送 means "to offer" (as a gift) but also "to deliver," which was of course the true meaning of the sign (although probably intentionally worded in an ambiguous way).

Deliberate ambiguity, a language problem, a question of face—it is up to you to judge which one applies to the situation you are in. In any case there will always be moments when you will feel totally lost. A foreign director confirms this:

"We were in talks with a Chinese official about organizing an event in Shanghai. I asked my assistant to give a full translation of what we were both saying. I'd hardly finished talking when my assistant took 3 seconds to translate what had taken the official about 10 minutes to say. I began to lose my patience: 'What are you doing? I asked you to translate everything he said.' She immediately replied: 'But I didn't understand a word he said. It was so ambivalent!'"

Make sure you have got a good interpreter when you are in negotiations with the Chinese.

Pretexts and excuses

The Chinese often come up with excuses and pretexts to avoid conflict. This practice is being more or less tolerated in Chinese society due to the fact that they facilitate and safeguard good relationships, harmony and face.

For instance, if a Chinese tells you that he will not be able to make it to your party (which had been planned and communicated for months) because something has come up, it may be his way of saying that he simply does not want to attend your party. He will try to avoid falling out with you and spare you from losing face. A fellow Chinese would have understood the allusion and the indirect manner of turning down the invitation. In general, the matter will simply be dropped.

An expatriate gives another example:

"My *ayi's* sister works for one of my French neighbors. Not long ago she told her:

—My mother-in-law is seriously ill. I must rush home because she is on her death bed. I can't say when I'll be back. I will have to stay home to look after my children.

—Okay, call me when you get back, said my friend who was deeply concerned.

Shortly afterwards, the *ayi* came to my door to see her sister.

When she left, I asked my *ayi*:

—So how's your sister's mother-in-law? Is she better now?

—Better? What do you mean? There's nothing wrong with her, she replied (clearly not knowing what I was talking about).

—Is your sister in Shanghai at the moment?

—Yes, she's working for an American family not far from here.

My friend was really disappointed when she found out and told me:

'I trusted her, I really believed her story. And to think I was ready to send flowers for the deceased.' "

To the French employer the story of the sick mother-in-law was an unacceptable lie, while the *ayi* simply wanted to avoid conflict and leave on good terms. Also, not telling her employer that she did not like working for her prevented the French lady from losing face. And on top of that the *ayi* saved her own face by avoiding being discredited on the market.

Pretexts are an everyday method of resigning in China. The Chinese manager of an *ayi* agency confirms this:

"A lot of *ayis* make up excuses for leaving. The family is the most common reason cited: mother, mother-in-law, father, grandfather, grandmother, who are either sick or about to die. Chinese families are perfectly familiar with these practices. If an *ayi* says something like: 'I don't know when I'm coming back, I'll call you,' this is a very bad sign. If she still doesn't know when she's coming back after three weeks, you'll never see her again."

This way of resigning or getting out of a work commitment often causes anger and disappointment among foreign employers, who always feel betrayed.

"What is used to protect the relationships for Chinese ends up destroying our trust in the relationships!" says a French sales director. He shares his personal experience:

"Rather than causing a loss of face, a Chinese prefers to make up a story. I still find this the hardest thing to accept in China.

For example, we decided to send our Chinese executives to France on a cultural management course to help them understand our habits and ways of working better.

Rather than telling me straight out that he didn't want to go on the course (for instance, by saying that he didn't find it interesting) one of my sales managers told me: 'I'm at a meeting in Paris the night before, I can't get to the course in Lyon the next day. There are no trains which would get me there on time.'

Now I am fully aware that the Paris-Lyon route is only 2 hours by fast train and that there are plenty of trains each day.

But I had learned my lesson, and rather than replying something like 'Wait a minute, you can easily find a ticket—stop talking nonsense,' I did it the Chinese way and said, 'Okay, let's leave it till next year then.' After all, I can't force someone to take a course against his will, but we both knew what was really going on."

Try to look at excuses and pretexts from a Chinese perspective. Consider it a way of avoiding conflict and maintaining friendly relationships.

In Summary

Ultimately, the Chinese are no more predisposed to lying than any European or American. It is just that they live in a culture where the notion of face is prevalent.

Remember that what you consider a blatant and hurtful lie is often a means of protecting face. Besides, they are not only worried about their own face—they also want to make sure you do not lose yours. So try to be patient.

Chapter 4: Brainteaser—Test your knowledge

True or false? Circle the right answers.

1. A Chinese person is capable of:

T/F: telling you something is red two days after saying it is blue.

T/F: telling you something is blue but with a touch of red, unless it is the other way around.

T/F: assuring you that something is blue even if it is quite obviously red.

T/F: telling you that something is whatever color you want it to be. *Mei wenti!*

Answer: Any Chinese is capable of giving you all of these answers. The Chinese are known for their flexibility, are they not?

2. True or false?

T/F: The Chinese always ask "Why?"

T/F: Westerners always ask "Why?"

Answer:

The Chinese rarely ask "why" because they fear it could be interpreted as an attempt to question the other person's word. Westerners on the other hand always ask "Why?" which will continue to baffle the Chinese.

While Westerners always try to establish a reason, the Chinese are more focused on relationships and face than understanding why something happened.

A European director says:

"When people first arrive in China, they often make the mistake of trying to understand everything. For me, what's important is fixing objectives and focusing on achieving them. You cannot spend your entire time trying to find out why things happened. In China that's impossible!"

3. **Which of these responses means "yes" and which means "no?"**

   a. Yes.
   b. No.
   c. I think it is possible.

   Answer:

   In fact, it does not matter if your Chinese counterpart says "yes" or "no," since a "yes" can mean "no" and a "no" is never definitive. What counts is not what is being said but the way it is being said. An "I think it is possible" in a confident tone is worth so much more than a feeble "yes" accompanied by a rigorous effort to avoid eye contact.

   A Chinese teacher explains how to tell the difference between a "yes" and a "no:"

   "When the Chinese mean "yes," they generally get on with things quite quickly. For instance, if you want a meeting with a Chinese person, he will immediately pull out his diary and suggest a date. If this doesn't happen then you are unlikely to obtain the appointment."

4. **Apart from *mei wenti* (no problem), which term do the Chinese use most often?**

   Answer: *keneng* (maybe).

   A European director gives an example:

   —Are you coming to the meeting?
   —Maybe.
   —So you're coming?
   —Maybe.
   —Yes or no!
   —Yes . . . maybe.

   I remember once asking a man who was selling DVDs in the streets: "Is this film in French?" His reply: "Maybe."

Chapter 5

Respect rituals and local customs

When you leave home, you ask the way.
When you enter a foreign place, you ask about the local customs.
Chinese proverb

Some people come to China with no interest in the country's rituals and customs whatsoever. After all, they came here to do business, not to conduct sociological research.

In a way, they are not so wrong. You do not need worry too much about respecting the rituals of the country since the Chinese are pretty forgiving in this respect. They usually will not make a fuss just because you did not follow their rules and traditions to the core.

There are cases, however, that will make the Chinese be much less accommodating. You can just about get away with forgetting to take off your shoes when entering someone's house (as is the custom) but other oversights, especially those related to the concept of face, can have serious consequences. Some rituals are an integral part of business relationships and it would be a mistake to underestimate their importance.

In any case, understanding and respecting a number of rituals and customs shows that we take an interest in the Chinese and their culture.

A French entrepreneur who was completely unfamiliar with Chinese protocol had a somewhat embarrassing experience:

"It was the first time that I had attended a banquet with senior Chinese business people. As a good Frenchman I raised my glass to a toast but I immediately realized that something was wrong. Everyone was staring at me and I suddenly felt very awkward.

This taught me about an important ritual in China: for reasons of face, it's always the most important person who raises his glass first."

This chapter is not about listing all the different rituals and customs that the Chinese follow so rigorously. As mentioned before, they are very forgiving when it comes to foreigners who make little mistakes with regard to Chinese traditions. We will therefore concentrate on those rituals and customs that are vital to saving the face of your Chinese colleagues or business partners and should therefore be respected and paid close attention to. In particular the rituals connected to dinner events and social gatherings are worth remembering.

A foreign sales executive attends several of these high class events a year. He sums his job up with a sense of humor:

"My job consists of buying and selling; of giving and receiving money; of drinking and eating. Those last two aspects are crucial to the prosperity of my business and require a lot more skills that one would imagine."

Politeness, rituals and the concept of face

It is helpful to consider the meaning of the word *li* 礼 (politeness) in order to understand the extent to which politeness and rituals are closely related. In fact, *li* also means: "ritual," "ceremony," "protocol," "etiquette," (*lijie*, 礼节, *jie* signifying the crucial moment) as well as "gift," (*liwu* 礼物, i.e. the object of the politeness). In China politeness is expressed more through the way you behave with respect to protocol and hierarchy rather than through verbal courtesies. Put simply, it is expressed more through actions than words.

Examples:
—A Chinese will not be particularly upset if you do not bother to say "Thank you" when being served at table. But he will be crestfallen if you refuse to try any of the dishes he prepared.

—The father of the family will not make a fuss if his daughter fails to say "Thank you." On the contrary, he might even be offended if she uses the expression "Thank you," as it is reserved for outside the home where relationships are not as close (a Chinese woman told me that after spending several months in France she automatically said "Thank you" to her father when he passed the salt which made him pretty angry).

Appreciating meals

You are the guest of honor at a business meeting and, as such, have the honor of being served first. Your Chinese business partners kindly turn the tray and wait till you have helped yourself to a portion of each dish before they help themselves. As an appetizer you are presented with a delightful porcelain dish loaded with chicken feet sporting delightfully curved claws, as well as mini-brochettes of silk worms. With visible disgust you decline: "No, no, thanks."

Then, the second dish is served. This time there are large shrimps wriggling around in a bowl of alcohol and you can already imagine them squirming about in your mouth when you bite their heads off. You pass the tray onto the person next to you saying: "No thanks, honestly," with a clumsy smile which fails to conceal your embarrassment.

While you are daydreaming of the delicious meal waiting for you at home, a portion of China's famous 100-year-old eggs is brought to the table (eggs preserved in a mix of salted earth and rice for several months, taking on a greenish color; not to be confused with 1,000-year-old eggs, a traditional Cantonese preparation which involves soaking eggs in horse urine). And of course everyone is staring at you to see how you react.

In China being a generous host is a way of giving face to your guests. Conversely, not accepting the meal can cause a loss of face to your host who has taken great care in selecting dishes for your pleasure. Moreover, the Chinese cuisine is known to be one of the best of the world. There are plenty of delicious dishes, even if some may look strange for you.

Nobody will blame you for not liking something after you have tasted it. The Chinese are aware of the fact that foreigners are unaccustomed to certain flavours, but categorically refusing the food on offer is considered extremely impolite.

So if you do not want to eat certain types of food, you can always make an excuse—such as "I'm allergic to eggs." The Chinese won't be fool but it's much better than saying "I'm not gonna eat that, are you crazy?" You can also follow the advice of this Chinese interpreter:

"Even if you don't like a dish, it is better to help yourself and then discreetly push the food to the side (mash with your chopsticks the helping slightly to make it look like you've tasted it). Note that it's not impolite to leave food uneaten on your plate and in fact it's better if your plate hasn't been totally cleared if you don't want to risk being offered a second helping! Some foreigners whom I accompany to dinners sometimes say 'No, no, I don't like it,' which really offends the Chinese."

Having said that, it would be reasonable to expect more understanding from the Chinese since, when it comes to foreign food, they are hardly best placed to be lecturing anyone. This story of a group of Chinese who refused to eat their meals in a prestigious French restaurant perfectly illustrates the point:

"A Chinese group launched a call for bids among major European companies. Known the world over for their exquisite gastronomy, the French prepared a meal in a classy restaurant in order to welcome the Chinese delegation with all appropriate pomp and ceremony. An entire dining room was hired and a menu painstakingly selected. Everything was prepared down to the last detail bearing in mind that the Chinese attach a lot of importance to this kind of event.

On the big day, the starter was followed by a main course of fish in a butter sauce. But all of the dishes had to be brought back into the kitchen because none of the Chinese had so much as touched it. Even worse, the Chinese delegation then asked the chef if he wouldn't mind boiling up some rice for them. Talk about a loss of face for the French chef!

Despite their best efforts, the French failed to win the contract. They would have done better to order some noodles* from a Chinese restaurant or even takeaway pizzas (it's worth noting that the Italians eventually got the contract)."

---

*   Note that the character *mian* of "face" is also used to designate Chinese noodles. A Shanghai restaurant specialized in pasta played on this double meaning to draw in customers by calling itself *you mianzi* ("to have face" and "there is pasta").

A French executive, who had worked in China as a trainee, remembers how little respect his Chinese flatmates paid the food he had so carefully prepared:

"After two months of living with two Chinese friends, I decided to treat them to a traditional French meal. I bought a bottle of red wine, some camembert and everything I needed to make fresh crepes (French pancakes).

I made around twenty crepes, or about six crepes each, as this is how much I would have expected them to eat. Turns out they only ate half a crepe each, which worked out at one whole crepe between them and 19 for me!

At least they drank the wine. In record time, I might add! After a couple of *gan bei** the bottle of fine French wine (which I'd purchased with my meagre savings as a trainee) was drained in no time.

Then came my grand camembert finale. I knew it was a bit risky, but I'd already seen them eating some sort of cheese made from milk curd.

Moreover, one of them was quite open-minded to foreign food. And yet he bit into a small piece of camembert and immediately spat it out onto the floor (while the second friend didn't even try it). I won't be cooking that kind of food again for Chinese friends, that's for sure!"

Apart from refusing to touch the food offered to you (and we can also add not leaving your chopsticks sticking out of your rice bowl since that is evocative of the incense sticks in rice offered to the dead), there are no real taboos.

As in a lot of other areas of life in China, at the table anything (or almost anything) goes. In fact, you can let out a few belches without the person sitting next to you raising an eyebrow; spit out gristle and fish bones onto the table or even on the ground (note, however, that at higher class banquets the leftovers are placed in a small bowl provided for this purpose), and you can chew noisily on your food with your mouth open or suck up your noodles with a slurp.

---

* *gan bei* is the drinking toast in China which literally means "dry glass."

In this respect the Chinese are far more lenient, as this French lady who is married to a Chinese points out: "It's easier for the French to learn Chinese table manners than for the Chinese to learn eating the French way."

On that point, let's me cite Lin Yutang in his book "The Importance of Living:"

"Why do the Westerners talk so softly and look so miserable and decent and respectable at their meals? I feel sure that the child gets his first initiation into the sorrows of this life when his mother forbids him to make noise when eating."

Although all of the cited in this paragraph is tolerated in China, you are not actually required to do it. In other words, do not force yourself to belch at the end of the meal, or slurp your soup noisily. This is neither required from a foreigner nor a Chinese.

At the dinner table you are allowed to do just about everything—except refuse to be served. Make up an excuse if you must.

The importance of *gan bei*

You are at a business dinner and a Chinese executive offers to fill your glass with rice wine so you can toast to the contract he is about to sign.

Well aware that this will be the first of many glasses you will be expected to down in one go and shuddering at the thought of ending up as drunk as the previous night, you tell him: "I don't feel great today. I think I'll just stick to water." Nice try but you may as well wave your contract goodbye.

It would not be surprising that your fellow diner simply moves across to another table where people know how to behave better (this actually has happened).

How many times have foreigners who work in China heard the cry of *gan bei!* The Chinese love to raise their glasses and they love it even more when you join them. As this French salesman testifies:

"When I first came here I used to lift my glass only to take a sip and the whole table would raise their glasses in a toast! I've since learnt to self-control!"

Another insight into what doing business with the Chinese can be like for the unwary comes from this young foreign manager:

"I'll never forget the first time I went to Yunnan province with a Chinese colleague. We had barely arrived and were already being seated for the evening meal. My colleague warned me that it was important to drink, otherwise our host would lose face. I wasn't that worried since I can hold my drink pretty well and like to party. But rice wine is like no other alcohol. I had to down this big glass and that's the last thing I remember from that night! The next morning I had the worst headache of my life and to top it all a builder was banging away at a partition in my apartment with a sledgehammer. It took me two days to get over this night."

If you turn down a drink, particularly in regions in Northern China, where the drinking culture is even more prevalent, your Chinese counterpart may feel like he has lost face. To refuse to drink may not be a problem in most Western countries, but it is certainly hard to get away with in China.

If your liver is hurting at the mere thought of drinking in China, the best plan is to work out a strategy to avoid excess consumption and limit the damage. Here are some of the tricks tried and tested by the many foreigners interviewed for this book:

- Ask for small glasses of alcohol so you drink less while face is saved.
- Drink plenty of water or tea between glasses in order to dilute the alcohol in your system.
- If you are in the rare position of being able to choose your own drink, opt for a beer (the second most popular drink in China after

tea). That way, you will still be relatively sober when everybody else is falling off their chairs.

- When your Chinese counterpart already has a reputation for being a drinker, you should arrange to meet over lunch rather than dinner. Generally speaking, less alcohol is consumed at lunchtime than in the evening and you will always have the excuse of having to go to another meeting.
- Tell them you are on antibiotics. They may not be fooled but at least that way nobody loses face. Mind you, your business prospects could suffer as a result.
- Do it like some of the Chinese—discreetly spit some of the alcohol into a napkin and, with similar discretion, ask the waiter to bring you fresh napkins at regular intervals.
- Order a glass of corn juice then spit some of the alcohol into the glass when nobody is looking. Some prefer to order orange juice for this purpose but corn juice hides it better due to its dilutive properties.
- If you are cornered, rather than obstinately refusing to drink, accept a few glasses. That way face is conserved.
- Under all circumstances make sure you have always got some aspirin or Alka-Seltzers with you so you can take it before going to sleep.

This discussion I recently had with a Chinese interpreter who often accompanies clients to official banquets, sums up the issues nicely:

> "You can't refuse to drink or say 'Honestly, just a little,' especially if the person raising his glass is a key player who attaches considerable importance to the idea of having a drink together as a sign of friendship.
> —So you just tell foreigners that drinking is mandatory?
> —No, but I do explain that in our culture it is a way of demonstrating friendship and mutual respect. I tell them that it's always best to go with the flow; saying 'no' is really bad for business."

Meanwhile for a Westerner, ending up drunk in front of a customer automatically causes embarrassement, many Chinese would view this type of behavior as a solid foundation for building a relationship of trust. Note, however, that getting sloshed at large and formal events will still be frowned upon. The best approach is clearly to find a way of matching the Chinese toast for toast without ending up under the table.

Never place your hand over your glass to refuse a drink—unless you have an <u>excellent</u> excuse.

Good manners

❖ The ritual exchange of business cards

On a business trip to China a foreigner meets a potential Chinese business partner for the first time. He reaches out and takes the business card offered by his Chinese counterpart without even glancing at it and then leaves it on the corner of the table. This seemingly trivial action will not have escaped the attention of the Chinese, who may take offense.

Being careless about the exchange of business cards is a serious *faux-pas*. The Chinese attach a lot of importance to this little piece of paper. Their face is reflected on the business card: their professional situation and titles reflect their social status. Not giving due consideration to the card presented to you amounts to not giving the person himself full consideration. This can be perceived as a loss of face, especially if you are dealing with a high-ranking player and others are watching.

An expatriate learned to keep a close eye on this detail:

"When I'm being given a business card by a Chinese, I always take time to inspect it: it's a chance to ask questions, take an interest in the individual, his title, etc. It's a way of giving him face.
This is a rule I always try hard to follow in China, something I didn't do systematically before I got here."

Technically you should exchange business cards holding the outer edges with both hands. This is a sign of respect. However, the Chinese are starting to pay less attention to this ritual. Sometimes, it is the other way round. Some foreigners living in China end up using both hands (even between themselves) and Chinese people working with them only use one hand. As a measure of precaution and in order to respect Chinese customs, however, it is still better to use both hands.

Take the time to inspect the business card that is being offered to you.

❖ Ritual gifts

Whether you are invited to someone's house for lunch, dinner or an after-school snack with the kids—it is only polite to bring something. Whether a fruit basket, sweets for the kids or a bottle of alcohol, all gifts are welcome (well almost all; refer to chapter 6 "Choose the right gifts").

If you fail to bring a gift, your host may think that you consider him unimportant.

A Chinese French teacher adds:

"If you arrive for dinner in France with nothing to offer to the hosts and try to apologize because you left work late and all the shops were closed you will be excused. It's the thought that counts. But to a Chinese, this would cause a genuine loss of face. You should have found a solution. There's always a way of buying or organizing something beforehand. You will not be forgiven."

Never arrive at your host's empty handed.

❖ Displaying affection

A Spanish businessman recalls one of his first trips to China:

"We were celebrating a Chinese colleague's birthday over a business lunch. Without even thinking, I leant across and gave her a peck on the cheek to wish her happy birthday. Big mistake! She turned bright red and everyone was clearly uncomfortable with the situation. I knew the Chinese don't kiss on the cheek when they meet but I had no idea that kissing a Chinese woman on the cheek could cause such a stir. I was told afterwards that this sort of thing was reserved for young lovers and even then it wasn't done in public."

Although this incident occurred ten years ago and some Chinese now peck their foreign friends on the cheek when they meet up, it will be best to stick to a handshake to start with.

Moreover, a man and woman who kiss in public are often considered to be behaving inappropriately (especially by older people). It is not only a loss of face for the kissing couple but also offensive for the others.

A Chinese lady who is married to a Frenchman says:

"When we were at my parents' house, my husband kissed me on the cheek in front of my little brother. My mother took me to one side and said: 'Your little brother is still young!' I should add that he was 20 at the time! The rule is that as long as children aren't married, they're still considered young."

Note that it would be forbidden to hold your spouse's hand in the streets, but anything more affectionate is considered to be ill-mannered.

Avoid kissing your Chinese female colleagues on the cheek, whatever the occasion.

❖ **Invite others to restaurants to give and receive face**

In a well-known French comedy sketch, a group of diners try to divide up a restaurant bill according to what each person had ordered. The reverse would be true in China. A similar sketch would show everyone fighting over the right to pay for the entire table to give themselves face.

A Chinese teacher confesses that she was surprised at the behavior of some of her foreign students:

> "Over the Christmas holidays my students invited me to a restaurant. Among them were some French and American expats. When the bill came they wanted to pay for me but I was really embarrassed when it took them ages to divide the cost of my tiny share by 14 people."

In China, dining out is a chance to give yourself face and give face to your guests. Also, the more expensive and sumptuous the dishes, the more face you give to everyone. Face is calculated based on the menu prices. A well-known Chinese restaurant even has an advertising slogan that says "We're the most expensive in Shanghai!" Face can also increase depending on which floor you are dining on in a restaurant. In certain Chinese establishments, the first floor is reserved for ordinary customers; the second floor is for VIPs; above the second floor is for VVIPs (very very important persons) and right at the top is where members of the government dine.

The experience of this European business man in China tells its own story:

> "In 1990 I was in a restaurant not far from Xian and as usual I was the only white person amongst about fifteen invited clients and their Chinese assistant. Her role was to select dishes for our guests, systematically choosing the most expensive (but note that what we might find not so expensive might still be very expensive for locals).
>
> When the waitress brought the bill the assistant snatched it from my hands and shouted: 'Oh, 3,500 RMB! But that's really expensive!'
>
> Everyone chorused: 'Thank you, thank you.'

When I told this story in Europe, people found it hard to believe."

In fact, most Chinese will not react this way but they will all appreciate the fact that you spent a lot of money on them.

Hence there is no question of splitting the bill in China. Either you pay the bill and your Chinese friend will invite you the next time around or vice versa. If you make too much fuss about paying the bill when he wants to pay himself you could cause him to lose face. You can always pay the bill next time.

> *Never pull out your calculator when you get the bill.*

In Summary

Ultimately, there are only a few rituals which the Chinese expect foreigners to respect, so you should always make the effort to play the game.

After all, you are in China!

Chapter 5: Brainteaser—Test your knowledge

Check the comments that apply to you:

- ☐ You cleared your plate the last time you were served chicken feet.

- ☐ You ended up drunk after a business meal more than once.

- ☐ Sometimes you make a fuss because you insist on paying the bill.

- ☐ You always bring a small gift when you are invited somewhere.

- ☐ You always have business cards with you.

- ☐ People who belch at your table do not shock you.

- ☐ You have already belched during a business meal.

- ☐ You always take off your shoes when you enter someone's home.

Result:

You checked all boxes:
You have perfectly adopted the customs of the country to give a lot of face to your Chinese business partners. However, try not to overdo it. Your liver's health and smooth reintegration back in your home country depend on it.

You checked at least 4 boxes:
You have assimilated several rituals and customs. Although you sometimes cause your Chinese counterparts to lose face, you make sure that local traditions do not encroach on your lifestyle.

You checked no boxes:
It may be that you only recently arrived in China, in which case you are excused. Otherwise you would do well to make more of an effort if you want to cultivate fruitful relationships with the Chinese.

Chapter 6

Choose the right gifts

A drop of water shall be returned with a burst of spring.
Chinese proverb

Someone once told you that offering gifts is a great way to build solid relationships in China. Since then you went out of your way to buy presents for all your contacts. That is a great first step, but you still have to choose your gifts very carefully and know a few basic rules to make sure your gifts give face and do not produce the exact opposite.

It was a copy of a luxury-brand watch that a busy foreigner had quickly purchased on a street market which ended up in the bottom drawer of a Chinese manager, who was shocked by this blatant lack of attention. The foreigner simply failed to understand that in China it is not just the thought that counts; the gift must also (and above all) meet certain criteria of face.

A European entrepreneur shares how easy it is in China to go wrong with a present and how he barely managed to avoid causing his Chinese business partners to lose face:

"We are trying to sell our products in the province of Anhui, so we organized a seminar in the region and invited Chinese companies with good business potential.
We prepared small gifts of baseball caps and key rings for everyone. Just before the seminar, we got to talk to some Chinese

who warned us in a very diplomatic manner that we should perhaps choose gifts which were "a little more appropriate" for "certain" investors.

Luckily there was an international supermarket nearby. We could save the day! So we raced into the store to find the best gift for the people who were seemingly more important than the rest. We ended up buying various French luxury perfumes.

When we offered the perfume to them, they inspected the packaging with an air of disappointment and all they could say was: 'Ah, it's not made in France.' (In fact the perfume <u>was</u> made in France but the product was packaged in China, a detail which we hadn't spotted). That was the only comment they made. We didn't even get a "Thank you" which left us wondering if it had really been worth all the trouble.

I noticed that the Chinese enjoyed the big, golden and glossy boxes, even tough the plainer boxes contained better quality and more expensive perfumes."

The debt of face

All relationships in China, whether professional or purely friendly, are based on a system of mutual debt.

Offering a gift, doing somebody a favor and, generally speaking, giving face to the other person creates a relationship based on reciprocal commitment. The recipient is obliged to reimburse his debt by offering the same thing or a service of equivalent or even superior value. If he is unable to do so, he risks losing face.

Illustration:

A foreign woman went all across town to help out a Chinese friend. Later that day the Chinese insisted that her husband should drive the friend home. Not realizing the importance of this offer, the foreign lady insisted on taking a cab. Only after her friend, who became increasingly irate, explained to her that it was her way of repaying a debt, that the lady finally accepted the offer.

So, in China friendship is not only based on a feeling of empathy and affection but also on the notion of returning favors. Thus, you can ask anything of a Chinese friend but they will also expect you to do the same in return. For instance, they could call you at the last minute to ask you to pick up one of their friends from the airport, which happened to a French lady at 5am in the morning.

Giving and receiving gifts

A European woman was very embarrassed when an elderly friend of her Chinese mother-in-law on a simple courtesy visit offered her son 200 RMB (20 euros/25 USD), roughly equivalent to the elderly lady's monthly pension. The European refused to accept such a sum, but her mother-in-law insisted: "That's how it works. Take the money or she'll get upset. Don't worry; I'll give her some fruit in exchange."

In China the act of giving and receiving gifts is subject to strict rules which you should be aware of if you want to avoid uncomfortable situations. All of those rules are directly related to the concept of face.

❖ Open the gift later

The Chinese have a rule which says that gifts should not be opened immediately. It is considered extremely rude to just tear open a gift (as it suggests that the recipient is greedy).

An embarrassing and somewhat comical situation caused by an unwary American in a Chinese family illustrates this further:

"During the Chinese festive period, my father's American friend offered my mother a ring. He wanted her to open the gift immediately.

As a mark of respect my mother felt obliged to wear the ring. But it turned out that it was too big for her and in order to prevent the American from losing face, she felt obliged to wear it on her thumb.

Embarrassed by the situation, the American suggested taking it back to the shop to get it changed but this caused even more embarrassment to my mother. She refused and decided to keep the ring as it was. In the end, everyone lost face.

In China this type of situation doesn't happen as it is the custom to open gifts after the guest has left the house, or else you're given money, which avoids these kinds of situations where everyone is ill at ease."

> ⬛ *Never make a Chinese open a gift in front of you, unless you are absolutely sure it is perfect for him.*

❖ The art of showing gratitude

Just as much as it is inappropriate to eagerly open a gift the minute you receive it, lavishing thanks is also frowned upon. The Chinese will perceive this as an attempt to ask for more—the contrary of traditional Chinese humility.

It is even considered polite to refuse the gift you are being offered (at least initially). This little cultural difference can lead to misunderstandings as this 80-year old Chinese charity worker discovered:

"The first time a foreign woman brought me things to give out to local people I said: 'No, no.' Seeing my discomfort, she didn't insist. She assumed I was genuinely embarrassed, turned on her heels and walked off with her box of clothes!

Had she been Chinese she would have insisted and I would have said something like: 'I'm not worthy of your gift, I can't accept it,' and she would have replied: 'But I insist,' and then I would have added: 'But . . . no, it's too much,' and she would have ended up saying: 'I promise you, it's nothing really.' Only then would I have accepted the gift, adding : 'respect cannot be compared to obedience.'

But now I've understood what to say to foreigners. When they offer me something I simply say 'Thank you,' and nothing else!"

You will never see the Chinese go into raptures over a gift. Nor will they thank you effusively. A Chinese may not tell you that he likes the gift but you can be sure that he will thank you another way: by inviting you to a restaurant, or by putting you in contact with someone, etc.

It is not necessary to thank the Chinese effusively when you receive a gift; a simple "Thank you" will do it. But make sure you return the favor at some stage.

Criteria for good gifts

Here are a few criteria to help you choose gifts and avoid the biggest *faux-pas*.

❖ **A good gift is one that is expensive**

Question: What is the most important criteria for a gift?

Answer: Its value. This is what a Chinese woman answered without hesitation: "For foreigners a good gift can be something small that comes from the heart. For us Chinese, this is not enough. It's the value that counts, which is why we will happily spend a fortune on gifts, particularly for close family members."

Foreigners can easily look like misers compared to the Chinese, who are extremely generous when it comes to giving gifts.

Chinese tourists in Paris devote much of their budget and time to buying gifts bearing the most exclusive labels. In fact, statistically they are in the process of overtaking the Japanese in their spending habits. This should speak volumes. Not that long ago it was not unusual for a poor Chinese family to risk financial ruin by buying gifts for a rich family which had invited them over during festivities such as the Chinese New Year or a wedding—all just to save face. A Frenchman gently mocks his Chinese in-laws: "My in-laws always bring us medicinal plants which are worth a fortune! We hardly dare touch them since they are so precious. They still have price tags on them!"

How well a gift is received seems to be proportional to the number of zeros on the price tags, which, as we have seen, some Chinese deliberately leave on the gift (of course if the gift is cheap nobody forgets to remove the price tag). A Chinese may be really offended by a gift which seems too cheap.

"What can sometimes shock foreigners who think that only the financial aspects counts, is in fact often a question of respect and face," explains a German. He shares his own experience:

"The first time I was invited to the home of my Chinese girlfriend's family, I brought everyone a gift: an enormous bouquet of flowers for the mother, some French cognac for the father, a box of Belgian chocolates* for the grandmother.

In Germany I would have felt ridiculous turning up with so many gifts. It would seem as if I were the future son-in-law going out of his way to impress the in-laws.

The second time I went there I brought a small album of photos taken at their home the first time, which I thought was a very nice gift. I was surprised when my girlfriend made a negative comment: 'That's not enough. It's very impolite!' I know my girlfriend really well and she's not materialistic like some women in Shanghai. However, for her it's very important to follow the rules. In China, a gift must be expensive. It's not just the price for the price's sake. It's more like the costlier it is, the more respect you show someone."

---

* I'm not sure whether the grandmother really appreciated the chocolates even if she gave no indication of her displeasure. Many Chinese do not like chocolate. I know what I am talking about because a Chinese friend regularly gives me all the boxes of chocolates that foreigners give to her husband. In fact, chocolates are usually reserved for children. For instance, a Chinese woman was shocked when her French in-laws brought a box of chocolates for an elderly relative in hospital: "Firstly, when someone is sick, you should give them healthy food, like a fruit basket, to make them strong. And secondly, chocolate, like all sweets, is for kids!"

> **STOP** *Do not minimize the importance of price when choosing your gift.*

❖ If it is not expensive it should at least be big

Small gifts don't exist in China. Even if Chinese modesty demands that you must always present your gift as "just a little something" (*xiao yisi*), do not take this literally. You can be sure that a Chinese who <u>really</u> only has a "little something" to give you, will not describe it as such.

If your gift is not expensive, it should at least be "big" or better yet, "grand." Gold wrapping papers and decorations, or gifts in huge and glamorous boxes are always appreciated. Take a basket of fruit for example. It is not necessarily expensive but it is always big and beautifully packaged. A massive bouquet of red roses and white lilies speckled with gold and silver will be perfect for Valentine's Day. The version with small teddy bears or little pink rats (stuffed toys I should add) in the bouquet is pretty good, too.

> **STOP** *If you want to avoid bankruptcy, go for cheap but large gifts with lots of glitter.*

❖ Do not make it too big or too expensive

An American decided to give a very special gift to a Chinese family during the Christmas holidays. He decided to offer his Chinese friends an enormous Christmas tree covered with glittering decorations. The perfect gift you might think: expensive, big and sparkling. Unfortunately, the tree was so big that they could not even get it into their modest apartment.

In China a gift must be big, but should not be too big, and it must be expensive, but not too expensive. It is all about finding the right balance. This is not only due to a problem of lack of space (which, by the way, should always be taken into account), but also and above all, due to the famous debt of face.

"If I give a friend who isn't particularly well off a gift which is too big, she could end up losing face," explains a Shanghai woman. "Next time she will be unable to offer me the same kind of gift."

In fact, offering an oversized or overly expensive gift can put a Chinese in an uncomfortable situation because they will feel obliged to "repay" their debt at some point.

Jean-Claude Peter gave an excellent example in his book "Comment Echouer en Chine" ("How to Fail in China"). Following an exhibition in Beijing, the head of a French association suggested giving as a gift to the Chinese authorities a herd of cattle brought over from France for the occasion, whose cost to return it to France would have been higher than the residual value of the animals:

"To their astonishment the French were informed that this was out of the question. The Chinese refused to accept such a sumptuous present. The French had failed to realize that in China, all gifts require a counter-gift of equal or greater value, or else serious face-loss incurs. And what could be offered in exchange for sixty highly prized cattle?"

The French ended up selling the herd to the Chinese at a low price, which helped reduce their debt of face.

(STOP) *Your gift must be expensive enough to give face but not too expensive to be repayable.*

Examples of good gifts

If you want to be certain not to go wrong, here are a number of gifts that will give face to their recipients.

❖ The "Number 1" gift: a bottle of cognac

"The last time I gave a bottle of cognac to a Chinese I made a friend for life!" says a young foreign business manager. In fact the bottle led to my first big business deal in China.

A bottle of cognac is the perfect gift but only the best will do—the XO grade: it is expensive and a typical product from abroad. In China these two factors go well together. Besides, it does not matter if your business partner has a whole collection of cognac—your bottle will always be welcome (a Chinese friend of mine has over ten of them on display in a glass cabinet in her living room).

A good bottle of cognac is a risk-free investment.

❖ Western products

The second most popular gift is women's perfume. Although the Chinese rarely use perfume, the Western cachet is sufficient to ensure the success of the gift. "Everything that is being made in Western countries is considered high value," says a Chinese lady who works for a French cosmetics group.

Perfumes, particularly the well-known brands, are preferred gifts. Lotions from major brands, silk scarves and handbags (only original ones please!) will also be greatly appreciated. Generally speaking, all luxury goods purchased in Europe will delight the Chinese. The Chinese also appreciate products which are typical in, or symbolic of your country of origin.

Famous Western products are always a big hit.

❖ The personalized gift

You can also opt for an original and personalized present, but it is always a little more risky.

However, the Chinese are often extremely touched by a small personal note. For instance, the photo frame offered by a foreigner when the wife of one of his suppliers has had a baby has been much appreciated. Similarly, a great book with beautiful photos can make a great present, provided you are familiar with your business partner's taste.

Yet, be careful about trying to play on individual tastes and preferences; you might be disappointed. An American businessman spent hours choosing a special and very expensive painting for a Chinese man he knew to be an art lover, but never knew if he liked the present or not, whereas a Chinese fresco with a dragon or tiger would probably have gone down better.

This sales director eventually learnt his lesson after several years in China:

"I used to put a lot of effort into giving high-quality gifts which were often very expensive, but they were not always fully appreciated. These days I don't go out of my way anymore and just offer the same gifts the Chinese give me: a Chinese horse painting (during the Year of the Horse), an enormous jade pig (during the Year of the Pig), a rooster-shaped object (during the Year of the Cockerel) etc.
However, I always make sure that I say a short speech when I hand over the gift. In my experience a little personalized speech is even more important than the actual present!"

So, when thinking about buying a gift, always remember that the Chinese remain conformist and often prefer a traditional gift to something original.

Go for original gifts only if you know exactly what the recipient likes. If in doubt, stick to safe bets.

Gifts to avoid

If you want to build and maintain friendly relationships with the Chinese read the following pages carefully.

❖ Low cost, run-of-the-mill gifts

Countless European and American companies give commercial calendars to their clients.

"A calendar is so ordinary and inexpensive," says a Chinese manager. "In companies, at least for executives of a certain level, it is advisable to invest a bit more in gifts. My rule of thumb is to spend at least around 300 RMB (30 euros/40 USD)."

If we are talking about special or famous calendars, or if the company's standing is high enough, that is another story. But most companies do not enjoy such a prestige.

The same goes for company diaries or planning books. An interviewee tells the story of a high-ranking Chinese man who was furious when a foreigner (who had lived in Asia for some time) gave him a small diary in the middle of a meeting. He was convinced it was a deliberate and vicious attempt to cause him to lose face.

In China, the more important the person, the better the gift should be. This is particularly true in the business world.

Avoid low-quality and mass produced gifts, particularly for high ranking individuals.

❖ Fakes

Counterfeits carry all the signs of a bad gift: they are cheap, made in China (not abroad) and so common for the Chinese.

The Chinese find it hard to understand why foreigners—who are supposed to have money—rush out and buy fakes. They just cannot understand why anybody who can afford it would buy fakes and not the original ones. The Chinese buy goods for reasons of face more than simple question of taste. In Europe or the United States it is often the other way round. You buy because you like something and if you can get it cheaper—even better!

This Spanish manager agrees:

"The Chinese I work with (who are all from Shanghai), can't understand why I would buy copies. They keep asking very personal questions which I still can't get used to, such as:
—How much did you pay for your polo shirt?
—Not much, 40 RMB. I got it at the street market, it's a fake.
—And your shirt? And your pants?
—All fakes.
I think to them there is a mismatch between the face I'm meant to have due to my social status and professional position and the face I show through my purchases.
Now when they see me with new clothes they smile and say: 'I bet it's a fake!' I think they find me very strange. To them I'm 'Mr. Fake.'"

Make sure you buy only originals.

❖ **Objects that bring misfortune**

There are gifts that you only have to mention and they already bring bad luck to you and your relationships.

Knives are such a case. While in Europe or the United States it is perfectly acceptable and even common to offer sets of knives to newlyweds or to customers, in China this would be a way of cutting off the relationship.

Most of us know that the Chinese are superstitious. Many superstitions are due to pronunciation similarities (for instance, the number 4 *si* is unlucky because it is pronounced the same way as the word for "death"). What is less well known is that the same circumstance is true for gifts.

We already mentioned the *san* (umbrella) which is pronounced like the Chinese word for "to separate." Hence an umbrella is never a good gift, but even less so when the gift is supposed to mark the start of a new business relationship.

Following up on the problem of offering knives, you should also avoid turning up with a basket of pears. Not only does the ideogram for the word "pear" contain the knife character (you have to cut it up to eat it) but moreover *li* (pear) is pronounced the same way as the verb for "to separate" or "to leave."

An even worse present, however, would be a clock *zhong*, which also means "the end of" or "being on one's death bed." In other words, it is probably the worst thing you can offer a Chinese. Americans in particular have a habit of offering newlyweds a clock, which is an excellent gift in the US. Imagine Chinese newlyweds who invite several Americans to their wedding, who all end up giving them a clock as a gift.

Improve your Chinese. It might come in handy next time you try to buy a gift.

The misadventure of this foreigner seems like an adequate finish to this chapter:

"A Chinese friend invited me and another friend to have lunch at a restaurant to celebrate the birth of his daughter. It was hard for us to decide what to give him as a present.

Something to wear maybe? But like us he worked in the fashion industry so he could probably get as much clothing as he wanted. Flowers? I was told that flowers weren't accepted in maternity hospitals since they can cause allergies. We knew that the Chinese often gave each other money (for example for the Chinese New Year or a wedding). So we decided to give money, which we put in a decorative red envelope as is the custom in China.

During the meal we placed the envelope on the table.

After five years in China it was the first time that I'd annoyed someone so much. I could tell immediately that we had caused him to lose face.

He returned the money by throwing the envelope on the table. Everyone was very ill at ease. We asked him:

—So what gift should you offer to celebrate a birth in China?

—A gold bracelet or a good luck charm, he replied, as if it were obvious. Then he added:

—What counts when you are born is happiness, not money.

How were we expected to know what the appropriate gift would have been? To our Chinese colleague, the fact that we hadn't even taken the time to ask somebody beforehand was inexcusable."

In Summary

The Chinese rarely forgive mistakes when it comes to their presents.

In China any gift offered is not only expected to match your business partner's taste but also to be aligned with face-related criteria. They expect every foreigner to know these things, so take it on board to avoid causing somebody to lose face. If in doubt, ask another Chinese for advice before giving out gifts.

Chapter 6: Brainteaser—Test your knowledge

Check the right answers.

1. **You are invited to the wedding of one of your employees. In the red envelope you should put:**

   a. 100 RMB (10 euros/ 15 USD)
   b. 1,000 RMB (110 euros/ 150 USD)
   c. 4,000 RMB (430 euros/ 570 USD)
   d. 250 RMB (27 euros/ 35 USD)

   Answer:

   —100 RMB is simply not enough. Even Chinese people with limited resources will give at least 200 RMB. If you do not give enough, not only do you cause the couple to lose face, but you lose face just as much by coming across as poor or stingy.

   —1,000 RMB is the minimum if you are the boss.
   A boss simply must give more than his employees. Also the closer you are (family, good friends) the more you are expected to give. The Chinese love even numbers (another sign of superstition since even numbers are evocative of a couple, 200, 600 . . .), so 1,000 RMB is a good figure. If you turn up without your family you can give a little less, maybe 800 RMB. Also, the number 8 will bring the newlyweds good luck.

   —4,000 RMB? Are you trying to cause the family to lose face or are you just determined to go bust? I can only hope that not all of your employees invite you to their wedding. Sums handed over at weddings are carefully noted so that at the next wedding, the same sum or even slightly more can be offered. Giving too much, as we have seen, may make the other person to feel they owe you an excessive amount of money. It can also cause a loss of face to other guests of similar standing who may have given less. A Chinese student remembers:

   "At my brother's wedding my parents gave him 500 RMB and my uncle, 1,000 RMB (In principle, close family is expected to give roughly the same amount). My parents felt they had lost face."

—Whatever the occasion, whether a wedding or any other important celebration, you should never give 250 RMB.

My own husband learned this the hard way when he first arrived in China:

"The day of pay increases, an employee came to me looking upset. He said: 'Look. I can't accept my pay raise.' A bit surprised I replied: 'I don't understand. I gave you a 250 RMB increase which is pretty good.' The employee replied: 'No, either you give me 240, or you give me 260, but 250 is impossible. You will cause me to lose face.' I hadn't been in China for that long at the time and wondered whether he was making fun of me. I talked to other Chinese to find out more. They explained to me that there is an expression in Chinese which says 'I give you 250' meaning 'I think you're a fool.'"

This has since been confirmed to me by other Chinese. Never say "*Liang bai wu*" (250) to a Chinese, it really is considered an insult.

2. **To celebrate the signing of a contract with a client you should offer him:**

   a. A clock to place on his desk because you noticed he does not own one.
   b. A bottle of cognac picked up at the airport in Paris.
   c. A company calendar.
   d. A small box of cheese decorated by your 3-year-old son.

   Answer: The bottle of cognac, of course!

3. **Your Chinese friends have just had a baby son. Which of the following gifts should be avoided?**

   a. Hard-boiled eggs painted red.
   b. Diapers.
   c. A small good luck charm.
   d. A fruit basket.

Answer:

The custom is to offer eggs painted red (eggs are excellent for your health when you are breastfeeding, apparently), but this tradition seems to be disappearing. I have, in fact, heard of a case where a Chinese employee asked her boss to buy diapers as a gift.

As we have learned in this chapter, money is completely out of the question. A good luck charm will do the trick (ask the Chinese sales assistant about which one to choose). When the baby is one month old, the custom is to offer a stuffed tiger which will serve as a toy and pillow and is supposed to protect the infant. When the baby is 100 days old, other objects are generally offered, such as long-life pendants. If you are really close, you could opt for a golden bracelet.

Finally, although the fruit basket is a good emergency solution when you are invited to someone's house, they are not offered to young mothers. They do not eat fruit for several months as it is considered bad for breastfeeding.

4. **You offer a gift to a Chinese customer. How can you tell whether or not he likes it?**

   a. He puts it in the bottom of his cupboard saying with a smile: "I'll only take it out for special occasions."
   b. He doesn't thank you but your sales with his company double the next month.
   c. Your sales with his company drop the next month.
   d. He is very ill at ease and refuses your gift.

Answer:

In China a good gift is put on display and shown off. So if a gift is condemned to the bottom of the cupboard, it is a bad sign.

The actions which your client will take in the future are certainly the best indicators. Doing business with you is a way of saying thanks, even if he has not put it into words. I am not trying to insinuate that sales are directly related to the gifts you hand out (this would be plain corruption) but it can certainly have an influence on the overall performance.

Finally, as mentioned in this chapter, your business partner's refusal does not mean he has rejected your gift, but rather that he is being extremely polite. However, you need to be able to distinguish between politeness and a categorical refusal. If you insist after a refusal, but your Chinese business partner continues to refuse after three attempts something is probably wrong with your gift. In that case reread this chapter to find out where you went wrong.

Chapter 7

Humor in China

*You never laugh as hard, long and loudly
as when you want to hide your pain.*
Chinese proverb

Surely you know somebody in your circle of friends or colleagues who is forever playing the comedian. He is the one who gets the whole table laughing over dinner and always has a funny story up his sleeve. However, what you and your friends might find funny could be terrifying for the Chinese. At best they may react with stony silence to your friend's jokes; at worst they will feel like they lost face.

Some people say that the Chinese have no sense of humor. It is true that the word *youmo* (humor) is a phonetic derivative of the English word*. It seems as if this notion simply did not exist in the past, but do not think for a minute that the Chinese are depressed or downbeat people. They love to laugh, have fun and make jokes—especially when time and place are

---

* The English word "humour" itself derives from the French word "*humeur*". "*Humeur*" designates the temperament or temporary state of mind which was previously attributed to the composition of the body's humours (originally a Latin word corresponding to bodily fluids) and which also took on the meaning of "a readiness to make jokes, and use irony" in 15th century France.

right, such as over a good meal. Moreover, the Chinese have a great sense of reality, or realism, which is part and parcel of their sense of humor.

But, sense of humor or not—Chinese humor is certainly not on the same page as European or American humor.

This Chinese lady's anecdote illustrates this point:

"I still remember my first month as a student in France and my first confrontation with French humor.

One day I'd just cleaned the floor of my bedroom in the dormitory, when a French friend came to see me. He walked in with his dirty shoes on. I didn't speak very good French at the time so I told him accidently: 'Take off your pants please.'

He replied with a wry smile: 'Not straight away.'

I was totally upset and humiliated and ran out into the corridor, because I actually thought he was being serious!"

Chinese humor

Chinese humor is mostly based on puns (hence the abundance of written humor and the need to be fully familiar with the subtleties of the Chinese language to understand), comic sketches (which often ridicule a problem) and satires (which mainly mock human stupidity).

Examples of Chinese jokes:

—A newspaper recently made fun of the Chinese people's growing fascination for money. They ran the following headline: *xiang qian kan* (there is a Chinese expression that says "looking towards the future" 向 前 看, which when written slightly differently but pronounced the same way means "looking towards the money" 向 钱 看).

—One day, a man went to see his doctor. Handing his patient the prescription the doctor said: "The effects of the medicine will last 24 hours." The next day his friends were starting to worry about him because he laughed for hours and hours. They asked him: "What's wrong with you today?" He answered: "The doctor told me to laugh for 24 hours."
"The effects of the medicine" is *yao xiao* 药 效 in Chinese, which can also mean you must laugh 要 笑. It is simply pronounced the same way.

—A Chinese drunk falls out a second-floor window. Passers-by immediately gather around the victim. A policeman arrives on the scene and asks: "What happened?" The drunk replies: "No idea, I only just got here myself!"

Go easy on irony

Irony, the notion of mocking somebody or making jokes at their expense is commonly used in many European countries. In the UK or France particularly, people make fun of each other (or themselves for that matter) all the time and their comments are rarely perceived as hurtful by their fellow countrymen. The Chinese have a very different attitude towards irony.

❖ Irony is often perceived as criticizm

"I've always loved using irony but I've totally given up this kind of humor in China! It doesn't work at all here!" says a French businessman.

He is absolutely right. Irony does not seem to have a place in Chinese culture.

At dinner with a mixed couple (French man and Chinese woman), we spoke about those minor intercultural obstacles. Our conversation went as follows:

Me: "What's the hardest thing about your relationship?"
She: "He's always making comments in front of others which make me look stupid and cause me to lose face."
Him: "But it's just to tease you! You know perfectly well that I don't really think it, usually quite the contrary. As we say in our country: "*Qui aime bien, châtie bien*" (Who loves well, punishes well)."
She: "Well, I don't think that stuff is funny."
He glanced at me with a mixture of surprise and amusement: "I had no idea it upset her so much. For me it's all just jokes!"
She ended : "From now on, you must avoid using irony in front of others, particularly when my hierarchical superiors are present!"

A Chinese teacher, who is an expert on humor in China, explains:

"For 2,000 years it has been unthinkable to make fun of the Emperor and any type of political humor was forbidden. One of the few recorded cases of irony dates back to the Second Emperor (the son of the first Emperor of the Qin dynasty, the one who left us with the famous terracotta soldiers, dating from around 200 years BC). When he raised the prospect of repainting the Great Wall, a minister told him: 'You're right, but why just paint it? Why not install a roof while we're at it?' It is said that the Emperor laughed out loud having understood the tongue-in-cheek nature of the comment.

But apart from exceptional cases such as this one, irony as a form of humor has no place in Chinese history or literature. When you pull a joke at someone's expense there's always a risk that they will be undermined and lose face."

Here are some humorous attempts which failed to produce the desired results:

A French woman tried to joke with her Chinese mother-in-law:

"One day when my husband was away, my mother-in-law prepared a special dish for me. In my usual frankness, I told her: '*Oh là là*! That's not the sort of thing I like.' I had already committed a cultural crime but the worst was yet to come.

She was surprised and replied: 'I don't understand, my son said you loved it.' I couldn't resist responding: 'He was probably thinking of another woman.'

She immediately flew into a rage: 'My son only has one woman in his life! How can you say that? That's totally unacceptable.' She added that I had caused the family to lose face and that I had offended its dignity. Thankfully my sister-in-law spoke my native tongue so I explained to her that it had been simply an off the cuff comment which was supposed to be funny, but it was impossible to get my mother-in-law to understand that."

On a lighter note, this joke happened in rural France:

"One day my husband drove off to visit a factory in France with some visiting Chinese colleagues.

He was behind the wheel and everyone was admiring the beautiful French countryside. The windows were rolled down so they could enjoy the view. Beautiful landscapes and cows grazing in meadows; consequently, some typical rural smells began wafting into the car. So my husband jokingly said to the person sitting next to him: 'It wasn't me!' The Chinese colleague sitting behind him exclaimed with obvious embarrassment and a degree of consternation: 'It wasn't me either, honestly!' The Chinese kept insisting so much that my husband ended up explaining that it was only a joke and that he knew that obviously the smell came from the cows. Yet the Chinese wouldn't let the subject go. My husband's comments were simply perceived as a loss of face."

A French lady almost started a street fight because she was trying to be funny:

"I went to visit a French friend in Beijing. She was known for her sense of humor and irony was her speciality.

We were on a tour of the Hutongs (old districts of Beijing) and had negotiated a rickshaw (bicycle-propelled taxi) for 150 Yuan. We stopped to visit a house and when we came out, another rickshaw owner offered to pick us up. Out of curiosity we asked his price. It turned out that he was willing to accept 130 Yuan, 20 Yuan less than the first guy.

As we were about to leave my friend turned to our guide and jokingly said: 'See that guy over there? He's cheaper than you!'

He immediately went over to the guy and starting shouting at him. Neither my friend nor I dared to say anything as the two men argued it out. What was meant to be a joke had now taken on amazing proportions. Would we ever be able to leave? A third person got involved, then a fourth who finally managed to pull them apart!"

> 🛑 *Make sure the Chinese know in advance that you are joking.*

❖ Certain subjects should not be joked about

"Sometimes foreigners crack the kind of jokes which really upset the Chinese, without ever realizing it," explains a Chinese manager. "This is of course true of racist jokes (where the Chinese are shown to be inferior to foreigners, for instance) and subjects related to poverty or the weakness of others."

A European student remarks:

"If I were to start laughing when seeing a short old lady in the street wearing a trendy T-shirt featuring the words "I love . . ." because it looks so out of place, my Chinese flatmate wouldn't laugh at all. If anything, he'd be offended and say: 'She's too poor to dress properly.' I used to try this kind of humor, but now I avoid it at all costs."

If you like making fun of your foreign friends' accents (my British friends for example, always laugh at my French accent when I speak English), it is best not to do this when it comes to the Chinese. They will take it badly:

"One day, my Chinese friend felt she had lost face because a French friend spoke in a Chinese accent to tease her. I did my best to convince her that it was just a joke!"

Sometimes, some foreigners go too far. Their attempts to be funny come across as sarcasm. A Chinese tells his story:

"We were having lunch at a factory with the director and a French buyer. When the director lifted the rice bowl up to his mouth as is the custom in China, the buyer burst out laughing and said: 'Ah, now I know why they call the Chinese rice bowls.' He couldn't stop giggling.
    I know he wasn't being nasty, since I'm used to working with the French and am beginning to understand their sense of humor. Luckily, the director didn't understand French, otherwise he would really have lost face.
    The buyer was laughing so much that the director ended up asking for a translation which nobody dared to give.
    After the incident, a Chinese woman who understood a bit of French took me aside and said: 'His comments were not very nice.'"

Avoid making jokes at the expense of other people (especially if they are Chinese).

There is a time for jokes

❖ **Know when to be serious and when to be funny**

The Chinese are often astonished to see foreigners cracking jokes in the middle of meetings when important subjects are being discussed.

"You can enjoy a good laugh in China, but only when the time is right. There is a time for laughing, which is generally outside of working hours, and a time to do your job and be serious," says a Chinese company manager.

"Outside of the official framework you can tell jokes," confirms a Chinese interpreter. "However, during official events, humor is not permitted." He remembers a French executive who made an enormous mistake:

"A major French group invited its Chinese shareholders to a special event. Over dinner, one of the French asked everybody to take part in a drinking song where you raise a glass to each part of your body before drinking it in one go. The big boss felt obliged to go first since he was highest in the hierarchy. He raised his glass from head to toe, passing it in front of his privates. He turned bright red in embarrassment and had clearly lost face in front of his entire Chinese entourage. It took at least three more dinners to make up for it!"

Do not tell your latest joke when you are in the middle of important business negotiations.

❖ **Dirty jokes**

Telling dirty jokes during a business lunch hoping to achieve some sort of male bonding experience with the Chinese is almost certainly doomed to fail. If the Chinese smile in such cases, it is probably out of politeness or embarrassment. Business meetings really are not appropriate situations for that sort of thing.

Not that Chinese men never tell dirty jokes (Chinese websites are full of them) but, like Chinese warriors, they choose the right time to strike. Generally that is at the end of the evening when the women have long gone to bed and the guys have had a few *gan bei* to help things on their way.

I had a conversation on this subject with an international couple (Chinese wife and French husband):

Husband: "There are two things I always avoid with the Chinese: jokes, and comments with sexual connotations. The few times I tried it I ended up being totally embarrassed. Yet the French love this kind of humor. In the beginning, my wife was really shocked to hear me using this kind of language and all, but she soon realized that everyone does it in France. Now she's more inclined to accept it even if she hasn't started telling dirty jokes herself!"

Wife: "Dirty jokes are considered extremely rude in China, especially in female company. It depends on the moment but in any case the window of opportunity usually closes fast."

Husband: "This kind of thing never comes up in meetings with the Chinese. But afterwards, when all the men get together for the karaoke, you might hear a saucy joke. That's the time to wheel them out. Then you feel more at ease with each other so the next day you might tease someone by saying, 'You were a lot more talkative at last night's karaoke!'"

Wife: "In fact, apart from these private moments such as at the karaoke, the Chinese almost never discuss sex. The French on the other hand always talk about it. What's that expression? There are those who talk about it and those who do it."

In China, with only few exceptions, you do not joke about sex. If in doubt, abstain!

❖ **Wait until you get to know people better**

Do not think that you have to give up joking altogether when you are in China. What might seem inappropriate if you do not know the person very well will be appreciated in the right company. For example, a French woman told me:

"My Dutch husband is very friendly with some Chinese people and makes vulgar jokes in front of them. For instance, one day he asked a Chinese friend: 'Where have you been? Not with your girlfriend again, I hope!' He replied: 'I was at the hospital taking care of my *xiao didi* (little brother).' My husband answered: 'Your stomach is so big you can't even see your *xiao didi* anymore' (note that *xiao didi* also refers to the male private parts). The friend wasn't remotely offended and the line even got a big laugh."

Note that Chinese people who are used to meeting foreigners often appreciate their sense of humor and find their fellow Chinese too serious by comparison. Several Chinese women even admitted falling for their foreign husbands because of their sense of humor.

Avoid testing your humor with Chinese you meet for the very first time.

Laughing to hide embarrassment

Although the Chinese have a tendency to take some of your jokes too seriously, you will no doubt be surprised to see them burst out laughing in situations that strike you as fairly serious.

Even if you know about this, watching Chinese giggle after they have been told bad news can be extremely confusing.

A European businesswoman tells the following story:

"I was flying back from Beijing with China Eastern Airlines. We'd been waiting for the plane to take off for ages. I asked the flight attendant what the problem was. At first she didn't even reply. She just walked off without giving me an explanation. Finally, she came back laughing her head off and telling me the flight was delayed for two hours! It was quite extraordinary and I remember feeling furious. A European flight attendant would certainly have used a more serious tone, something more appropriate to the situation. She would have probably said something like: 'We apologize for the late departure etc.' For the Chinese on the other hand the only way to reassure passengers and disguise her discomfort was to start laughing."

A foreign boss admits that he was enraged when his Chinese employee had a fit of giggles:

"Our products had been held up at customs for three weeks. The Chinese simply refused to let them in.

I said to my assistant:

'We can't go and see the customer without the products. The problem must be resolved. Can you take care of things?'

My assistant simply said: 'Okay.'

Then I discovered that customs had already sent the products back to where they had come from. I immediately contacted my assistant who was meant to keep me up to date.

She started laughing with her hand over her mouth.

—What's so funny? I said.

She carried on laughing.

—It's a very serious matter and I for one am not laughing.

She started laughing even more, which of course made me even angrier! At that point, I thought to myself: 'I don't believe it! She's making fun of me!'"

You probably wonder why on earth people would laugh in such situations. The answer in one word: face. It is not that your Chinese counterparts are failing to take you or the situation seriously, but simply that they are trying to conceal their embarrassment. When the Chinese do not know how to react or feel cornered, they laugh. It is what is known as the "bitter laugh" (*ku xiao* 苦 笑) in Chinese. The Chinese never laugh so much as when they are losing face!

The type of laugh can also speak volumes about the degree of face lost: it goes from a slight, embarrassed snigger to a barely stifled and convulsive laughter to a hearty guffaw for the really serious situations.

After having worked with the Chinese for five years, this Spanish company manager came to the following conclusion:

"When there is a problem, the Chinese I do business with have an annoying tendency to laugh. At first that made me furious, but now I actually think they've got it just right. What's the point of getting all worked up about things? There are plenty of problems around, so it's better to tackle them with a smile!"

If a Chinese person laughs when faced with a problem, just smile.

In Summary

You can let yourself go and give full vent to your humor if you know your Chinese counterpart well and especially if he is already familiar with the Western sense of humor.

However, try to avoid risqué subjects in female company. Also never make fun at the expense of other people.

And, if you see a Chinese laugh in extremely serious situations, instead of wondering what is so funny, consider whether you may have provoked a loss of face.

Chapter 7: Brainteaser—Test your knowledge

Check the right answers.

1. **What is the best adjective to define Chinese humor?**

   a. Non-existent
   b. Incomprehensible
   c. Untranslatable

Answer:

—Non-existent? If humor is restricted to irony and tongue-in-cheek comments, then you could almost argue that there is no such thing as a Chinese sense of humor. However, Chinese humor does indeed exist. The Chinese are pretty jovial and often ready to laugh out loud. They see the humor in most things as long as there is no face at stake.

—Incomprehensible? For non-Chinese speakers, that is highly likely.

—Untranslatable? Chinese jokes are often hard to translate because they use a lot of puns. Sometimes there are simply no equivalents in the respective language. When I was looking for examples of jokes based on puns, some Chinese friends sent me a humorous poem written in Chinese characters. When I asked them to translate it, they said it was impossible. Thanks anyway!

2. **What kind of humor strikes you as the most appropriate at dinner with Chinese?**

   a. This is a French joke about Belgium: a Belgian is driving down the motorway. He turns on the radio and hears: "This is a special announcement! We have just been notified that a car is driving down the motorway on the wrong way. Be on your guard!" The man turns off his radio, looks around and says: "No kidding, there are hundreds of them!"
       (Taken from: www.humor-blague.com)
   b. The last joke a Chinese told you (and which you understood).

c. A riddle.

d. None, because you never know—the Chinese might take it the wrong way.

Answer:

To be avoided: the Belgian joke and the riddle.

I told this Belgian joke to my Chinese friends. They did not laugh at all. Most could not understand why we would make fun of Belgium and would lecture us, saying: "The face of another country is extremely serious!" Or, "The French seem to want to humiliate the whole world." A joke between people from Marseille and Paris would perhaps have worked better. People in Shanghai, for instance, are always joking about people from the province of Jiangsu. It's better you avoid making jokes about foreigners (except maybe if you are making fun of the Japanese!).

You are taking a big risk when it comes to riddles. A Chinese interpreter, who was accompanying a group of French and Chinese ministers, remembers when one of the French businessmen told a riddle: "The Chinese minister felt he had lost face since he didn't know the answer! Of course the French were not expecting the minister to respond because it was just a game (after all, the comical effect of the riddle is based on the surprising answer, which is almost impossible to find)."

Chapter 8

Humility is King

All nobility springs from humility.
Lao Tzu

Being overly self-confident or even arrogant towards the Chinese is certain to cause significant face-loss as well as failure in your business. China is a massive market with great business opportunities, but if you want a piece of the cake it is paramount to remain humble at all times.

Nobody is safe from this particular pitfall. Which one of us, in a moment of impatience or fatigue perhaps, has not behaved in a way the Chinese interpreted as condescending?

Living in China is one big learning curve, as the case of this young French woman shows:

"I recently went to the opera and all the way through the performance a Chinese man in his sixties constantly rustled a plastic bag in the seat behind me.

French people love preaching to others, so I felt like asking him to stop. At first I turned around to him and put a finger on my lips saying, 'sssh.' Then, after he kept being noisy, I respectfully asked him to stop making so much noise. Following several other fruitless attempts to get him to be quiet, I finally snapped and tried to grab his bag (not too violently I should add).

Although he had failed to react up until then, he suddenly went into a rage, leapt to his feet and started shouting at me (right in the middle of the opera). At the interval he almost struck me and said in English: 'You should apologize to me.' I'd never seen a Chinese so angry!

To my mind, making so much noise during a live performance shows a total lack of respect. But for him, as a young foreign woman, I was the one showing him a lack of respect.

What this incident taught me is that we both attached importance to respect—except that we had a different approach. Not only did he not understand my viewpoint, but I had also caused him to lose face."

Chinese humility

To the Chinese modesty is the noblest of all virtues.

People who want to be the center of attention, who shoot from the hip and impose their ideas, are not those who succeed in China. Individuals who are able to demonstrate humility usually fare best.

The proud goldfish—a Chinese children's story:

In a pond there once lived a goldfish whose wavy tail was beautiful to behold. "Little goldfish, how rapidly you swim. You are faster than a running deer!" said a frog. "Little goldfish, how elegantly you swim. More elegant than the flight of the golden phoenix!" said a crab. Upon hearing these compliments the little goldfish nodded his head, shook his tail with joy and, believing to be superior to all other creatures, began to treat the others with contempt. He said to the frog: "Off you go! I am as beautiful as the deer but who looks at you, you ugly thing!" Then he turned to the crab: "Off you go! I am the golden phoenix but who looks at you, how clumsy you are!" Finally he declared to the whole pond: "I don't want to live here anymore!" So he summoned all his strength and leapt out of the pond. "Look I'm flying," said the goldfish, his heart filled with pride. He had hardly finished speaking when he fell to the ground and died.

Who knows where those who approach China and the Chinese with arrogance will end up?

Warning:

Skip the following pages if:

— You have just had a dispute with a Chinese.
— You cannot handle criticizm.
— You have been driven crazy by building work starting at 6 am in the morning (on a Sunday!) and are now holding it against every Chinese that ever lived (and God knows there are plenty of them).

Arrogant foreigners

A Western human resources director tells this story:

"In a company where employees are paid an allowance to buy mooncakes during the mid-autumn festival, a foreigner openly declared: 'They're such a pain in the neck with their cakes. And those cakes don't even taste nice!' The Chinese who overheard his comment were furious and asked the company to publically make it a formal rule that at each automn festival, mooncakes are distributed this way to restore face."

Some foreigners who come to China are so full of themselves that they will get Chinese customers to move in a restaurant so they can take what they consider the better table (unbelievable but true). Fortunately, these ill-mannered individuals remain in the minority and, in any case, are barely worthy of our attention. These people would often behave similarly in their own country and are usually the same ones who moan about their business interests failing to take off in China.

A Chinese manager says:

"It's not because you're from a developed country, earn more money and have, in theory, been better educated that you have the right to look down on others.
Personally, when I observe certain foreigners enter the country convinced of their superiority and starting to give out orders in

an arrogant manner, I prefer to avoid doing business with them. I already know that relationships with them will eventually turn sour. To avoid losing face the Chinese are ready to give up all sorts of things, including contracts.

You may hold all the strong cards but if you don't take time to show people some respect you are sure to fail sooner or later."

There are also those who take on some sort of superior air the minute they arrive in China. It is worth remembering that the privileged foreign status (the Chinese give enormous respect to all things that come from abroad, including you) can go to the heads of some foreigners, who get so used to the VIP treatment that they actually start believing that they are somehow inherently more important than anybody else.

This foreign manager is well placed to discuss this topic, having seen a steady stream of new arrivals to China over the past 20 years:

"We sometimes have a tendency not to put China on the same level as developed countries, which leads us to making mistakes of which we are often not even aware. For instance, someone walks into a meeting. He introduces his compatriot but omits to introduce his Chinese assistant!

The Chinese are extremely sensitive to attitudes and external signs (gestures, facial expressions, etc.) which might suggest that you are treating someone as inferior (they wonder: 'if I weren't Chinese, would he still be talking to me like that?').

If there's one word of advice I would give to foreigners arriving in the country for the first time, it is to demonstrate that you consider yourself to be at the same level as your Chinese business partner."

There are also those who turn up in China with plans to change everything. They impose their ideas and methods which they automatically assume to be superior to those of the Chinese.

"When you arrive here the initial instinct is to say that it's a complete shambles," says a human resources director. "Of course China is not structured the same way Western countries are. In China, things are always round or oval but never square. You just have to accept that. The Chinese have found their way of succeeding and they're currently proving it to the world. The first lesson you should learn in China is to challenge your own certainties and ways of doing things."

The comments of a European director setting up a branch in China are a nice conclusion to this point:

> "I sometimes get the impression with our head office that if the Chinese do the job it does not have the same value as the work done by their own staff. Yet there are some highly competent people in China. It's really irritating for my Chinese personnel to feel that we treat China like an underdeveloped country. It's important to remember that it's the second biggest economy in the world!"

Stop considering China an underdeveloped country.

Preachy foreigners

Our tendency to preach (French and Americans especially can be guilty of this) is often grounds for a loss of face. We constantly bring up censorship, human rights, poverty levels, in short, all the topics guaranteed to offend the Chinese. It definitely does not mean that we have to keep silent about these issues just because the Chinese may lose face, but rather that we should take into account the cultural sensitivity.

Indeed, the Chinese are highly sensitive to criticizm directed at their country. In fact, China is like one big family. Even more than national pride, the Chinese have a common bond based on a strong sense of belonging and cultural identity. They defend their nation's face just as much as that of their own families.

Although nobody likes hearing negative things about their home country, for the Chinese any such criticizm is also perceived as a loss of face. And they can react furiously, as this Englishman found out over dinner:

"Over dinner at a friend's house we got onto the subject of the media and disinformation in China.

My friend's Chinese wife got absolutely furious and said to her husband: 'You know perfectly well that's not true! The same thing goes on in your country, where the media also put their own spin on information.' I'd never seen her so worked up.

I realized there was no point continuing this discussion and quickly changed the subject."

Here is another account:

"During a trip to Tibet with some French people and a close Chinese friend, we got talking about the Chinese government and freedom of speech. We were just wondering whether the Chinese could criticize their government in the same way as the French so readily criticize theirs.

We asked him for his opinion, but my Chinese friend (who is normally very open-minded) clammed up completely and angrily retorted: 'You don't like China! You're always criticizing it! That's not what China is like at all.'

That was the end of the discussion."

A Chinese manager says some foreigners should avoid making unfair comparisons. He tells how a European caused a face-loss both to him and the director of the plant that they were visiting:

"Some buyers who visit China start off with questions like: 'Do any children work in your plant?' 'Are workers fed properly?' (As if there were no other interesting questions to lead off with in asking about the plant).

One day one of them even insisted that the plant director should allow him to go and see for himself what the workers were eating. In France it may be unacceptable to serve workers a bowl of rice with a small portion of vegetables and meat, but in China this is a standard meal."

While it is undoubtedly important to defend the values we cherish, there are diplomatic ways and means to convey our ideas. Trying to impose our practices without taking into account the cultural context should strike everybody as inappropriate and ineffective. It would be unreasonable to expect a canteen in the deepest region of China to serve the same quality food as a French or German canteen.

The intentions are generally honorable as was the case with a foreign lady outraged at meal times in an orphanage when she saw babies being laid across laps and spoon-fed rice. She expressed her indignation in a meeting with the director of the establishment. It seems that even if the *ayis* are sometimes a bit brusque and have to work fast, this way of force feeding infants, which tend to shock foreigners is simply the way babies have been fed in China for generations. All she achieved was to cause the director to lose face and worsen relationships between the orphanage and outsiders.

Under the guise of good intentions and defending our values we often feel that we have the right to sermonize and demand that others behave the way we do.

A Chinese woman says:

"The French often highlight what goes wrong in China. When we speak about France, we don't focus on riots in the suburbs. That's your business, not ours."

Or as the Chinese proverb would say, make sure you clear the snow from your own doorway before you start complaining about your neighbour's frozen roof.

So if you want to talk to the Chinese about their country, focus on the pleasant things. For instance you can talk about Chinese cuisine and the places you have visited in China. If you are really interested in the country there are plenty of topics. The 2008 Olympic Games or the World Expo 2010 in Shanghai, both sources of immense national pride, provide for a great opportunity to give your Chinese business partners face, although that largely depends on how you raise the subject!

Do not behave like you are trying to save the world.

Shocked foreigners

Many foreigners are astonished by certain types of behavior in China which they often see as a lack of respect. It is curious to observe that what we consider a lack of respect in turn causes us to behave disrespectfully towards the Chinese and cause them to lose face.

Foreigners are often shocked to see the Chinese spitting in the streets. Yet they do not realize that their comments or reactions can cause the Chinese who are accompanying them (and who do not spit in the streets) to lose face.

A Chinese translator shares an experience:

"We were in a taxi with some foreigners. The driver spat out of the window and immediately the foreigners gave full vent to their disgust. I felt I'd lost face and offered them my excuses for the driver's behavior."

Moreover your appalled expression will do nothing to change the person's behavior because they consider it perfectly normal. In fact, ejecting phlegm through the mouth is what most Chinese doctors advise. It is therefore a natural gesture in China, although better educated Chinese don't spit in the streets and recognize the hygiene problem it poses. It is also worth noting that the number of people spitting in the streets has fallen dramatically, particularly in large cities such as Shanghai and Beijing, especially since the SARS epidemic, for hygiene reasons and in the run-up to the 2008 Olympic Games, for image reasons. Remember too, noisily blowing one's nose into a used tissue as foreigners sometimes do, is quite as much disgusting to the Chinese.

The lack of interest in their fellow citizens that is quite noticeable when you use the public transport or walk in the streets is another type of behavior.

I had the following conversation with a Chinese manager:

Q: Foreigners are often shocked by certain behaviors and expressions of indifference which they observe in the streets. For example, if someone falls off his bike, there are plenty of people standing around staring but nobody feels like helping. It seems so harsh sometimes, that I've already heard some foreigners wonder if people here actually have feelings!

A: It's true that if there's an accident in the street nobody seems ready to offer assistance. This happens all the time.

Q: Why do you think that is?

A: It's not part of the Chinese mindset to lend strangers a hand. There is no notion of assisting someone in danger, neither in the law nor in the culture. Moreover, there are cases when people who have tried to assist have then been found responsible for what happened, making them liable for costs. There was a case here recently of a man who jumped into the water with a mobile phone in his pocket to save someone from drowning. He then asked the person he rescued to replace his broken phone, which the person refused to do. This illustrates the way of thinking on both sides. The case ended up in court and the rescued had to pay 1400 yuan (140 euro/190 USD or one month's salary) to his rescuer. In China, people think twice before coming to someone's aid.

Q: Are there other reasons for this behavior in your view?

A: When you give something you normally expect something in return. That's part of the Chinese mentality. This explains why we take care of our nearest and dearest and pay less attention to strangers.

Becoming involved in someone else's business can carry enormous risks. Moreover, it is through adaptation to their environment and self-protection, rather than a lack of community spirit, that the Chinese sometimes seem indifferent to the fate of strangers. They have an obligation to prioritize care for their immediate entourage (family, friends, company and social network) and for those people the support is quite extraordinary. Having said that, the Chinese showed an amazing community spirit after the massive earthquake in 2008 which seemed to have had a great emotional impact on the whole country. There have also been numerous cases of inter-company solidarity. So the community spirit does exist, but it focuses more on those who are considered to be part of the same family.

Try to look at beyond the perspective of the street.

In Summary

If the concept of face had to be summed up in a single word, that word would be "respect." Even if we do not always have the same ideas about what constitutes respect, we do share the same underlying principles. Always try to be humble and remember that we are merely guests in China.

Chapter 8: Brainteaser—Test your knowledge

Circle the answers which best correspond to your reactions:

1. **What is your attitude to spitting?**

   ☐ If there is one thing in China you cannot stand and will never get used to, it is spitting.

   Δ You don't take it seriously. Instead, you are reminding the joke that your friend told you: did you know that the Chinese have just placed a special order for aircraft? Two accessories were added to the cockpit: a horn and a small opening on the side so the pilot can spit out.

   ○ It does not bother you anymore as long as it does not land on your shoes. There are limits after all.

2. **Your TV broke down and the repair man you called has been unable to fix it:**

   Δ You smile and think about the Chinese forks you bought the other day which bent in two the last time you tried to use them, laugh it off and think: "made in China."

   ☐ You lose your temper with the repair man. That fact that your TV broke down is obviously the fault of the Chinese.

   ○ You tell yourself he is only trying to do his job.

3. **You come across an article in a magazine describing the long hours Chinese children spend doing their homework:**

   ☐ You feel revolted because making children study so hard is simply inhumane.

   ○ You have no judgement to make.

   Δ You smile and think "These Chinese are crazy!"

4. **You are out shopping. You are interested in a souvenir but the price asked by the shop assistant is way too high:**

   ○ You haggle and enjoy the experience as much as the seller does.

☐ You hate haggling because you always get the feeling that you are being ripped off. You end up losing your cool and yell: "Why did you say 300 to begin with when you're ready to accept 100 now?"

Δ You tell him with a smile that you could have 10 identical souvenirs for that price.

5. **You see the Chinese worker you hired to install something trying to climb out your window:**

☐ You wonder why he did not plan his working schedule better to avoid having to sneak out the window.

O Nothing surprises you anymore. One method is as good as another.

Δ You find the whole situation comical and say to yourself: "Everything is possible in China!"

Results

If you have a majority of ☐:

Think of the last time a Chinese person reacted badly to you and ask yourself why. Could it be because you adopted a negative attitude from the start? According to experts in intercultural management you are in the midst of a culture shock (which starts after one to two years for those working in China and after just a few months for those who live there but not working). Do not worry: it usually goes away after a while. Take the test again in a few months.

If you have a majority of △:

You are starting to take things as they are by using humor. Excellent, you have understood that there is no point in getting worked up. But do not overdo it or you may end up crossing the line and start to become sarcastic.

If you have a majority of ◯:

You know how to adapt to cultural differences. Although you may still commit a couple of cultural mistakes like anyone else, your attitude is generally respectful and this has certainly allowed you to avoid causing face-loss on numerous occasions. Well done!

A little test to finish:

Without removing the tip of your pencil from the paper try to connect all points using just 4 lines (passing across each point only once). You have 15 minutes to find the solution.

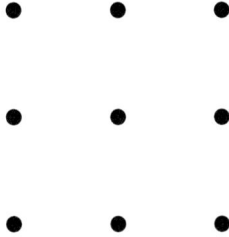

```
●     ●     ●

●     ●     ●

●     ●     ●
```

Solution:

Think outside the box!

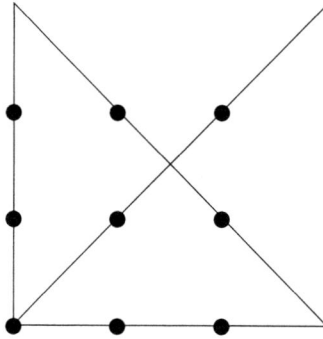

Did you find the solution? Well done! We often remain boxed in our limited mindset which prevents us from looking beyond our prejudices and own set of values.

You gave up before the 15 minutes were up? Try to be more patient—it could come in handy in China. As the saying goes: "With time and patience, the mulberry leaf becomes silk."

Conclusion

I hope that in my own modest way I have contributed to the development of the understanding, respect and openness towards those who do not necessarily work or think the same way you do, or share the same values.

I also hope I have provided some insight into the concept of face which will facilitate your contacts with the Chinese, as well as your personal and professional life in China.

But enough words for now, as the Chinese proverb says: "Speaking does not get the rice cooked." It is now up to you to behave in a way which does not cause the Chinese too much loss of face.

I will close this book with a quote from former UN Secretary-General Kofi Annan:

"Cherish your individuality, respect the individuality of others and constantly seek out common grounds rather than division. It is up to each and every one of us to nurture the dialogue of civilizations."

Bibliography

Chinese Business Etiquette (Scott D.Seligman—Warner business books)

Les miroirs de la négociation en Chine (Marie-Chantal Piques—Editions Philippe Picquier)

La pratique de la Chine (André Chieng en compagnie de François Jullien—Grasset)

La Chine et les Chinois (Lin Yutang—Petite Bibliothèque Payot)
(My Country and My People—Lin Yutang)

Comment échouer en Chine (Jean-Claude Peter—L'Harmattan)

China Streetsmart (John L.Chan—Pearson Education)

Acknowledgements

My heartfelt thanks go to all of you who believed in this book and made space in your often busy schedules to share your experiences with face. Your personal insights, your examples, your stories, indeed all of your contributions have proved invaluable and make the richness of this guide. I hope that I have faithfully recorded your comments.

Many interviewees were keen to stress that their comments and anecdotes should not be taken as criticizm of China, since they think highly of both the country and its people. I hope that the spirit of respect in which I wrote this guide meets their expectations.

About the author

Anne-Laure Monfret is a management and human resource specialist who lived in China for eight years. Born near Paris, she attended business school and later was a management consultant with a firm specializing in Human Resources. Along the years, she developed a deep interest in cross-cultural issues. She has written numerous articles for magazines in China and elsewhere, and lectured on the key cultural notion of *face* at the French Chamber of Commerce in China and at international business schools.

She has two young sons and is currently living in Mamaroneck, New York. She divides her time between journalism and the writing of a new book related to China. She plans to return to Shanghai in the fall of 2011 for lectures.

CPSIA information can be obtained at www.ICGtesting.com
Printed in the USA
BVOW001203200513

321167BV00001B/3/P